D0006010

EVERYTHING!

PARENT'S GUIDE TO

CHILDREN WITH SPECIAL NEEDS

Dear Reader,

Having a child with a special need has very different considerations now than just a few decades ago.

Today's child with a special need is engaged in activities and learning with his family, his school, and his community. He is likely to be included in a regular school classroom with his peers for part or all of the day. He may participate in community sports and extracurricular activities. Someday, he may work at a job that will follow employment guidelines set forth by the Americans with Disabilities Act.

More than ever before, society is ready to embrace the unique talents and abilities your child has to offer. Parenting your child requires many hats—decision maker, provider, advocate, encourager, disciplinarian, teacher, confidant, and friend.

I hope this book will provide ideas and information that will help you raise a wonderful child who happens to have some special needs.

Lynn Moore

To my family, thank you for your encouragement and support.

An Everything® Series Book.
Everything® and everything.com® are registered trademarks of F+W Media, Inc.

Published by Adams Media, a division of F+W Media, Inc.
57 Littlefield Street, Avon, MA 02322 U.S.A.
www.adamsmedia.com

ISBN 10: 1-60550-163-8
ISBN 13: 978-1-60550-163-5

Printed in the United States of America.

J I H G F E D C B A

Library of Congress Cataloging-in-Publication Data
is available from the publisher.

This publication is designed to provide accurate and authoritative information with
regard to the subject matter covered. It is sold with the understanding that the publisher is not engaged in rendering legal, accounting, or other professional advice.
If legal advice or other expert assistance is required, the services of a competent
professional person should be sought.
　　　　—From a *Declaration of Principles* jointly adopted by a Committee of the
American Bar Association and a Committee of Publishers and Associations

Many of the designations used by manufacturers and sellers to distinguish their
products are claimed as trademarks. Where those designations appear in this book
and Adams Media was aware of a trademark claim, the designations have been
printed with initial capital letters.

This book is available at quantity discounts for bulk purchases.
For information, please call 1-800-289-0963.

All the examples and names used in this book are fictional,
created by the author to illustrate the key points of information.

THE
EVERYTHING®

PARENT'S GUIDE TO
CHILDREN
WITH
SPECIAL NEEDS

A reassuring, informative guide to your
child's well-being and happiness

Lynn Moore

Aadamsmedia

Avon, Massachusetts

Contents

Introduction

A ll parents share similar dreams for their children. They want them to be successful at what they do; they want them to be happy. Above all, they want them to be healthy.

With scientific advances, the medical needs of more infants are being identified prior to or just after birth. According to the Centers for Disease Control and Prevention, in the United States one of every thirty-three babies is born with a birth defect. Some of these children have conditions that can be corrected with surgery or therapy. Others will have ongoing special needs throughout their lives.

Many parents undergo a seemingly uncomplicated birth experience. The preschool years may bring few, if any, concerns about their child's development. With the start of school, though, comes struggle after struggle learning the basic ABCs and math skills. Often after attempts to help with schoolwork, referrals, and evaluations, a learning disability is discovered. The U.S. Census Bureau reports that 11 percent of children between the ages of six and fourteen have a disability.

Changes in education legislation have brought new, long overdue opportunities. The Individuals with Disabilities Education Act (IDEA) and No Child Left Behind Act (NCLB) remind schools and parents of their responsibility to challenge every child, and to provide the experiences and education needed for them to perform as closely as possible to their nondisabled peers. Many children with special needs continue their education through the postsecondary level.

Advocacy groups have worked to increase awareness of the needs and talents of children with special needs in school and in recreational activities as well. A child with a special need is often as involved in community and recreational activities with friends who do not have a disability as he is in activities designed to meet specific needs. No longer is a child separated because of a special need. In many instances, that same child is the star of the team or leader of the student body. Fellow students and peers in the community are growing up with an understanding that a disability does not mean lack of talent or incapacity to contribute to the group.

This new awareness of the abilities of individuals with special needs has now spread to the workplace. Employment laws have changed; fair employment practices are now mandated by the Americans with Disabilities Act (ADA). This legislation and higher levels of training or education make working more realistic for many. The community is seeing individuals with disabilities in a new light, as contributing members of society.

The task of parents of a child with special needs is to guide their child in choices that offer quality of life in all areas: medical, educational, recreational, and employment. In addition, parents must plan for their child's future. Living arrangements, insurance, and long-range financial planning are needed.

In many ways, parenting tasks are the same for every parent. Parents of a child with special needs face the extensive decisions that all parents must make, but there are many, many more to get to the same goal . . . a successful, happy child.

The goal of *The Everything® Parent's Guide to Children with Special Needs* is to support parents who are facing uncommon decisions with information and ideas that can help them make the best choices for their child.

CHAPTER 1

Discovering a Special Need

According to the Centers for Disease Control and Prevention (CDC) website (*www.cdc.gov*), "birth defects affect about one in every thirty-three babies born in the United States each year." Not every birth defect is life-threatening, and not every birth defect is detected at birth. However, every parent's heart breaks for a child who has extra obstacles to overcome in life. A baby's special need affects herself and every member of her family.

Hopes and Dreams

From the time a couple discovers they are going to have a baby, they begin to dream about the baby's future and how her birth will impact the family. Perhaps the parents' hopes and dreams are not as obvious as hoping their daughter will become a doctor or a lawyer, but the hopes and dreams are there. Many parents never think that there is a chance that their baby will have a birth defect. Unless there has been some indication that the pregnancy is not going well or there is a family history of birth defects, parents assume that their baby will be healthy . . . ten fingers, ten toes . . . a happy, healthy bundle of joy.

Although parents hear about babies with congenital defects, it seems like something that cannot happen to their family. When they learn that their baby has a birth defect, a number of emotions and reactions can follow.

Much research has been done on parents' reactions to the news of a child's disability, and most special educators agree that each parent reacts differently. Parents are as unique as each of their children.

Some parents react with doubt or disbelief . . . surely it cannot happen to their child. Some parents become depressed. Some experience guilt, feeling that they must be to blame. Others become angry, believing that their child's disability must be someone else's fault. Reactions and feelings can be mixed and can change over time. Hopefully, the parents will accept their child's condition, and with acceptance comes the ability to address the child's needs realistically.

Genetics and Family History

Some special needs are the result of genetics and can be traced through family medical history. Many times though, parents are unaware of the risk of their child having a birth defect.

Birth Defects Found in Extended Family

A birth defect might be passed on from previous generations, although it might not be immediately recognized as such because it does not show up in Mom, Dad, or even grandparents. Hemophilia is a condition that can be passed on by a baby's mother although she has no evidence of the condition herself. Because it is conveyed through the X chromosome, her sons have a chance of manifesting hemophilia.

Birth Defects Due to Autosomal Recessive Inheritance

Perhaps both parents have the recessive gene for a particular disability. Any of their children who receive recessive genes from both parents will have the condition or disease. There is a 25 percent chance that a baby whose parents both have a recessive gene for a condition will manifest that condition.

 Essential

Folic acid (a B vitamin) is helpful in preventing brain and spinal column birth defects often referred to as neural tube defects (NTDs). Because this part of the baby's body begins to form early in the pregnancy, the CDC recommends that women of childbearing age get 400 micrograms of folic acid daily.

Examples of autosomal recessive inheritance conditions include cystic fibrosis, PKU, galactosemia, sickle cell disease, albinism, and Tay-Sachs disease.

Birth Defects Due to Autosomal Dominant Inheritance

Some birth defects result from inheriting a single, dominant gene. If one parent has a dominant gene for a particular condition or disease, it may be passed on and manifested in the child. Marfan syndrome, Huntington disease, and at least one form of dwarfism are examples of autosomal dominant inheritance.

Genetic Counseling

Couples planning to have a baby may seek genetic counseling. In fact, usually early consultation with an obstetrician-gynecologist will include completion of a questionnaire on family medical history. If there is an indication that genetic risks exist, it is critical to seek more extensive genetic counseling. Such counseling might include asking extended family members to complete health questionnaires or certain medical screenings and lab tests for one or both parents.

Environmental Factors

We live in a society of increasing concern for the environment. Our concern, of course, is for a safe world for future generations to live long and healthy lives. Undoubtedly, some birth defects are caused by environmental factors.

Most parents today are conscious of the effects of lead exposure to the cognitive and neurological development of a child. Lead-based paints have been replaced with more child-friendly kinds.

Medical history has shown the impact of immunizations, lack thereof, or use of certain medication on the health of unborn children. Some present-day groups advocate avoiding immunizations. However, the risk that a baby will contract a disease if the mother is not immunized is serious and can be life-altering or even life-threatening. In the late 1970s, the United States saw an increase in the number of children with hearing, vision, and heart defects. These children were referred to as babies of the rubella bubble. Because their mothers had not been immunized for rubella and contracted the disease during their pregnancies, the babies were born with defects in larger numbers than seen in the general population.

The thalidomide babies of the late 1950s and early 1960s are a horrifying example of the effects from a prescription drug taken by women during the early part of pregnancy. Prescribed for morning sickness, the drug resulted in the absence or malformation (shortening) of limbs of many of these infants.

After the Vietnam War, babies were born with orthopedic, mental, and vision defects due to exposure of their fathers to Agent Orange.

Today, the effects on unborn children of other agents such as pesticides, preservatives, and food dyes are cause for concern. Research is being conducted on many fronts with the understanding that children are not immune to their environment.

Prenatal Tests

Birth defects are often detected prior to a baby's birth through advanced medical procedures: ultrasound, lab tests, prenatal screenings, and diagnostic tests. The doctor may increase the number and type of tests based on genetic history, the mother's health, or her age.

 Alert

There is a certain level of risk with invasive prenatal tests. Talk with your doctor about the reasons for the testing and the possible risks to you and your baby. Only you and your doctor have the information to make the right medical decision for you.

Your doctor may choose to conduct one or more ultrasounds during the course of your pregnancy. According to the U.S. Department of Health and Human Services website (*www.hhs.gov*), an ultrasound is effective in detecting many of the major birth defects, including neural tube defects such as spina bifida and anencephaly. Certain blood tests are more effective in identifying Down syndrome.

Your doctor may order lab screenings or diagnostic tests that will indicate the risk of certain conditions. Diagnostic lab tests offer more specific information about whether or not the baby actually has a certain condition. Amniocentesis and chorionic villus sampling (CVS) are two of the most common diagnostic tests used during pregnancy.

Newborn/Infant Screenings

Even with medical advances, many birth defects go undetected or may not be detected with certainty prior to the actual birth. In some cases, the parents may have been given the level of risk for having a baby with a particular condition or defect. The time of the baby's birth and the following days may be the time the baby is diagnosed.

APGAR

The APGAR is the first test given to newborns. It rates the baby in five areas: (A) activity, (P) pulse, (G) grimace, (A) appearance, and (R) respiration, thus its acronym—APGAR. Hospital staff will give your baby a rating (0–2 points) in each of the areas when he is one minute old and when he is five minutes old. The purpose of this test is to see how the baby tolerated his birth and how he is adjusting to the world. If there is concern regarding the baby's rating, he may be evaluated again at ten minutes of age.

Newborn Blood Tests

Your hospital will take a tiny amount of blood from your baby's heel to test for several birth defects. They will test for PKU (phenylketonuria), hypothyroidism, galactosemia, and sickle cell anemia. However, some states run as many as fifty tests on newborns. Most of the tests check for the baby's ability to metabolize food or milk. Without the ability to do so successfully, a baby can become retarded or even die. Often when a condition that interferes with metabolism is identified, it can be corrected with diet and/or medication.

Newborn Hearing Tests

Many states screen newborns for hearing loss. A small probe in the ear canal or an electrode on the head is used to transmit sound. If the baby does not show an adequate response, he will be referred for more advanced testing by a pediatric audiologist. Being referred for additional testing does not mean that the baby has a hearing loss. It is, however, important to follow up with the testing. It is critical for a baby with a hearing loss to be fitted with a hearing aid at a young age when speech and language skills are developing.

 **Question**

How can I find out which tests my state runs on newborns?
The National Newborn Screening Status Report lists the tests run by each state—including the name and abbreviations for each condition it is testing. The report indicates if a test is required by the state. In some cases, a test is available but must be requested.

Something's Not Quite Right

You may have suspected that something is not quite right regarding your baby's development. Perhaps she is not your first child. Perhaps she is not quite keeping up with the milestones in the baby books and magazines. Perhaps you just have that gut feeling that only a parent can have.

Developmental Milestones

Click on a reputable website such as the March of Dimes (*www.marchofdimes.com*) or Parents as Teachers (*www.parentsasteachers.org*) to see a breakdown of developmental milestones by month. You will find information on a baby's development in several areas:

- Gross motor skills (crawl, sit, stand, walk)
- Fine motor skills (grasp an object, manipulate a shape puzzle, pick up an object)
- Speech skills (coo, babble, say single words)
- Vision (focus on parent's face, follow a moving object with eyes)
- Hearing (turn head to sound)
- Social skills (smile, make eye contact, accept hug)

Not all babies follow the developmental milestones timetable. Some babies develop sooner, and some take longer, especially if born prematurely. However, sometimes a delay in reaching a developmental milestone indicates a special need.

Siblings and Other Babies

Comparing your baby to others is good and bad. It is helpful to have a reference, but you do not want to judge your baby's development strictly by what another baby is doing.

Remember that babies do not all reach developmental milestones at the same time. On the other hand, if you see a significant difference between what your baby is doing and what other babies the same age are doing, it is wise to discuss your concerns with your pediatrician.

Well-Baby Visits

Regular checkups or well-baby visits with a pediatrician will give parents the opportunity to discuss developmental questions and concerns with a knowledgeable professional. If you did not choose a pediatrician prior to your baby's birth, it is important to establish that relationship before you take your baby home from the hospital.

Well-Baby Visit Timing

Your pediatrician will outline the timeline for your child's well-baby visits. According to The March of Dimes, parents can expect the visits to be at approximately the following ages:

- One to two weeks after birth
- Two months
- Four months
- Six months
- Nine months
- Twelve months

- Fifteen months
- Eighteen months
- Twenty-four months

Do not be alarmed if your pediatrician follows a slightly different schedule. The important thing is to find a pediatrician and adhere to his guidelines.

Well-Baby Visit Objectives

Pediatricians have certain objectives for well-baby visits. According to The March of Dimes these include:

- Charting growth
- Physical examination
- General development
- Nutrition
- General discussions
- Tests
- Immunizations

As important as the other objectives is the discussion with parents. This is the time to ask questions and discuss your concerns.

Well-Baby Visits for Infants with Special Needs

Some babies are known to have extreme or complicated needs from the start. A general pediatrician may feel confident assuming care of the baby, while specialists address more specific health needs. Perhaps a child with club feet would be seen by a general pediatrician as well as an orthopedic doctor. If the doctor does not feel confident treating your child, contact the nearest children's hospital for a referral to a pediatrician who specializes in treating babies with special needs.

Preschool/Kindergarten Screenings

Some kinds of special needs are not identified during infancy. Learning disabilities, some kinds of hearing and vision impairments, and some behavioral problems may not show up until the later preschool or early elementary years.

Parent-Infant Educators

The term *parent-infant educator* can refer to a professional who works with typically developing babies and their parents, or someone who works with babies with special needs and their parents.

Parents as Teachers is a nationwide program that provides in-home instruction for families with typically developing babies and preschoolers. A trained professional explains the developmental milestones for the children in the family based on their ages, and will demonstrate developmentally appropriate activities for parents to do with their young children. Families can also participate in parent group meetings and screenings to monitor their child's overall development.

Early intervention is the term used to describe therapy and education services for children with special needs in the birth-to-age-three range. See Chapter 6 for more information.

Preschool Screening

School districts offer free preschool screenings in cooperation with their special education services. Preschoolers (age three to five) are tested on motor skills, speech and language, vision, and hearing. If there appears to be a significant delay, the child is referred for further testing. If hearing or vision is the area of concern, the child is first seen by a doctor to determine if there is a treatable medical condition. (For example, a child with a hearing loss due to fluid in the ear from an ear infection may have normal hearing once the infection is treated.) Testing may also be completed by an audiologist or school psychologist.

Early Childhood Education

Prior to age three, a child with a special need might receive services from appropriate therapists based on her Individualized Family Service Plan (IFSP). This plan is developed by the family and a team of developmental specialists. When the child turns three, an Individualized Education Program (IEP) may be written by the parents and a team of school personnel. An IEP outlines goals, accommodations, and modifications to meet the child's unique educational needs. The IEP replaces the child's Individualized Family Service Plan.

Other Preschools

In some cases, a child's special need might be discovered as he attends a traditional preschool program. He may even be a part of a universal preschool program, a program to boost the academic and social skills of children from the lower and middle class.

Kindergarten Screenings and Beyond

Some school districts offer a kindergarten screening in addition to preschool screenings. During a kindergarten screening, the child may be evaluated for gross and fine motor skills as well as cognitive development as they pertain to kindergarten readiness.

A child with any type of special need is best served through early services. In many cases getting help early on is all he needs in order to participate in a typical education program.

Determining that there is a special need is an important first step, but it is just the first. Once you verify that there is a special need, you face the question: Now what? You will have the challenge and privilege of introducing your baby to the world. As his parent, you are his best advocate and first teacher. Read more in Chapter 10.

You will also have lots to do on the home-front for your baby, your family, and yourself. Develop a plan of action that includes five basic parts: therapies, education, networking, day-to-day business, and personal care. The following chapters of this book will help you get started.

CHAPTER 2

Defining Special Needs

Many conditions, illnesses, and injuries can result in a disability or special need. Some affect a single area: physical, sensory, cognitive, communication, or emotional/behavioral. However, many children have multiple impairments, due partly to modern advances in medicine that push premature babies' survival rates beyond the dismal odds of previous generations. It is important to remember that the *special need* of a particular child is as unique as the child herself. Use the following definitions as starting points to learn how to interact with, challenge, and motivate the wonderful child in your life.

Developmental Delay

Developmental delay is the term used to describe a child's significant lag behind peers in physical, communication, social, or cognitive skills. Often the emphasis is on cognitive ability or a combination of skills.

In some states, every child with a special need is said to have a developmental delay until age six, regardless of an obvious condition such as blindness, deafness, or cerebral palsy. The rationale is that other disabilities may also be present, and singling out an area of need too early may cause something to be overlooked. By age six, professionals have a more thorough understanding of how the child functions in all areas.

Illness, injury, complications at birth, genetics, and unknown factors can result in developmental delay in a specific area (such as cognitive skills like mental retardation) or delay in a combination of areas.

Down Syndrome

Down syndrome is one of the most common examples of developmental delay. This condition is the result of an unusual chromosome split; a child with Down syndrome has forty-seven chromosomes instead of forty-six.

The physical characteristics of a child with Down syndrome include slanted eyes, somewhat flattened face, one crease across the palm of the hand, and low muscle tone. A child with Down syndrome is more likely to have medical problems, including hearing, vision, thyroid, heart, and general infections. As far as behavior, a child with Down syndrome may characteristically be loving and yet very stubborn.

Physical Disabilities

Physical disabilities include a wide variety of conditions that affect a child's movement or ability to accomplish some physical task. A physical disability might be a condition that is addressed with physical therapy or some assistive device, or it can be serious enough to be life-threatening.

Neural Tube Defects

Neural tube defect refers to the malformation or absence of some part of the central nervous system (the spinal column and brain). *Spina bifida* is one kind of neural tube defect in which an opening remains in a baby's spinal column. Spina bifida can result in full or partial paralysis of the legs. *Anencephaly* is the other major neural tube defect. With this condition, a part or all of the brain does not develop.

Cerebral Palsy

Cerebral palsy is a condition that refers to a lack of muscular control because of a breakdown of communication between the motor control centers of the brain and the muscles of the body. A child with cerebral palsy may have difficulty walking or using her arms and hands to complete everyday tasks. As with most disabilities, cerebral palsy is manifested in degrees. Some children have milder symptoms and may walk with leg braces or crutches. Others have a more severe form that results in limited use of all of the limbs. Cerebral palsy can occur while the child is still in the womb. In some cases it develops or becomes evident during birth or infancy.

More Physical Disabilities

Some babies are born without limbs or with limbs that are not fully formed. Sometimes this happens because of a genetic factor; sometimes this is a result of medication taken by the mother during pregnancy; and in some cases, the cause is unknown.

Other physical disabilities are caused by illness. Juvenile arthritis, muscular dystrophy, and cystic fibrosis are a few debilitating illnesses in children.

Physical defects can also be caused by injury. As with every type of special need, a physical disability can be acquired at some point in childhood (or adulthood). Children with orthopedic disabilities usually receive physical and occupational therapy to help them learn strategies for everyday life.

Speech

Parents tend to put as much emphasis on their baby's first word as they do on the first time he takes a step. Remember that the speech milestones are guidelines. Not every baby begins to use single words (or sentences) at the same age.

Normal Speech Problems

Sometimes parents are concerned about speech problems that are actually temporary, normal, and unavoidable. A common concern is when a child in early elementary school is not able to pronounce the *s* or *th* sounds. Because children of this age lose their front teeth, and front teeth are needed to make these sounds, the problem is unavoidable—at least until the permanent teeth grow in.

 Alert

Speech represents a child's understanding of language and his ability to use it. Speech and language are necessary to function in life, and begin to develop very early. Contact your doctor with concerns about your baby's speech development. A true speech delay can be caused by many things (medical or developmental) and should be addressed as soon as possible.

Physical Disabilities and Speech

Some speech problems have a physical cause requiring intervention. Before surgery, a child with a cleft palate does not have the closure of mouth and lips needed to make all speech sounds. Other children have difficulty because of the structure of the tongue and lips or the ability to use them correctly. Some children cannot speak properly because of problems with tonsils, adenoids, or severe allergies.

Impact of Other Disabilities on Speech and Language

Very often, disabilities don't show up alone. Speech and language difficulties are not uncommon tag-alongs with other kinds of special needs. Many children with developmental delay or learning disabilities have difficulty with language. They may show delays in understanding vocabulary or in putting words into sentences.

In many instances, these children do not understand what is being asked when questioned. When asked *what* they ate for lunch, for example, they may respond by explaining *where* they ate. In some cases, they do not understand that the speaker is even asking a question that requires a response.

 Essential

Work with your child's speech and language therapist and his teacher to monitor the time he misses class to attend speech therapy. Speech and language are critical skills, and yet there is a time when the effects of missing lessons in reading, math, and science outweigh the benefits of continued speech instruction.

Selective Mutism

Some children are physically able to speak, but do not do so. This may take place in all areas of the child's life or only in a few places (at school or in large groups). There are several possible social or emotional factors that can cause selective mutism.

Hearing Loss and Speech

Hearing loss impacts a child's speech and language. He cannot say what he has not heard, or he says something in a way that he *has* heard it—possibly missing or substituting some sounds according to the loss.

A hearing loss that affects speech may or may not be permanent. While some children have a permanent hearing loss, others have fluctuating hearing loss that can be caused by fluid in the middle ear. This fluid can be the result of ear infections or allergies. If a child has frequent ear infections, he may be missing valuable words and language.

Hearing Loss

There are degrees of hearing loss, determined by several factors. Some people with hearing loss can't hear sounds below a certain volume or outside a certain range of frequencies or pitch. Some hearing loss even comes and goes. If your child has a hearing loss, talk with her audiologist or teacher of the hearing impaired to better understand the type of loss she has and how the loss will impact her ability to hear in different situations.

Some hearing loss is considered to be in the hard-of-hearing range. A child who is hard of hearing has functional hearing of some of the sounds used in speech. With a hearing aid, she may be able to understand all or most of what someone is saying, providing that there is not a lot of background noise.

Deafness

Children who test in the range of deafness do not hear speech sounds, but many of them have *some* hearing. Perhaps they can hear a few loud environmental noises with a lower pitch. A lawn mower, a plane passing overhead, and a motorcycle are examples of environmental noises that fall into this range.

Cochlear Implants

Some hearing-impaired children are candidates for cochlear implants. In the past, a child would only receive an implant for one ear. With medical and technological advances, many children now receive bilateral implants (on both sides).

A cochlear implant involves a surgical procedure. Electrodes are implanted into the cochlea of the ear. A receiver is also implanted behind the child's ear. When the child wears a specially programmed microphone and speech processor, sounds are sent electronically through the implant's components. A child with cochlear implants will need considerable training in understanding and using these sounds.

Unilateral Hearing Loss

Sometimes a child has a hearing loss in only one ear, which is referred to as a *unilateral hearing loss*. It may be partial or a complete loss. Usually she will not have speech problems related to the hearing loss because she has "normal" hearing in the other ear.

There are some cautions that come with a unilateral hearing loss. Be aware of your child's safety and communication needs. For example, in a split second, a child can be headed for a dangerous situation (touching a hot stove, running toward a busy street, climbing on unsafe surfaces). Be aware that she may not be able to hear you if you are calling from the side of the hearing loss. Instinctively, you should position yourself on the side of her good ear to maintain safe communication.

 Essential

Be willing to share information about your child's hearing loss (even if it is mild or affects only one ear). If teachers, activity leaders, and child care workers are unaware, the result can be a dangerous situation for your child. In learning situations, preferential seating will ensure that your child is not missing out on valuable information.

A unilateral hearing loss impacts communication in other situations as well. Conversations and following directions can be difficult. If the person speaking is talking to your child's bad ear, she will not know that she is expected to respond or follow a direction. This can result in the appearance that she is uncooperative.

Central Auditory Processing Deficit

Some children have characteristics of hearing loss, but have normal hearing. They may not be able to understand what is said in a noisy classroom. Even in a quiet room they may have difficulty if the teacher is reading a spelling list of words with similar sounds or giving a list of instructions for an activity. A child with these characteristics may have a *central auditory processing deficit* (CAPD).

A central auditory processing deficit can look like other disabilities (hearing loss or attention deficit), so testing by an audiologist is necessary to diagnose this condition. If CAPD is indeed the problem, the audiologist may suggest that your child wear an FM auditory trainer or that speakers be used in your child's classroom.

Assistive technology is not always the answer for a child with central auditory processing deficit. Often, a reduction of classroom noise or the repetition of the instructions (or having the child repeat them) is helpful.

Visual Impairment

The eye is a complicated sensory organ. A child's ability to take in information through sight is important for mobility, safety, performing tasks, and learning (i.e., following classroom presentations and reading textbooks). Some types of visual impairment, such as nearsightedness and farsightedness, are relatively mild and can be corrected with glasses. Other visual impairments are more severe and require surgery, special education, and classroom materials.

Low Vision

A child who has *low vision* has only partial sight (even with eyeglasses or surgery). Low vision can be the result of illness, injury, or a condition since birth. Children with low vision may need adapted materials at school (books on tape, large print, or raised-line paper) and instruction in mobility training, at least at the beginning of a new school year.

Legally Blind

A child's ability to see falls on a continuum. Some children can see well without glasses. Others have some vision impairment (low vision). At another point in the range, a child is considered legally blind. The American Foundation for Blind defines *legally blind* as having 20/200 vision or less with correction in the better eye.

 Essential

Boost your child's self-esteem through communication with other children who are blind. A free, Braille pen pal program (Braille Slate Pals) for children in kindergarten through twelfth grade is cosponsored by The National Organization of Parents of Blind Children (NOPBC) and the National Federation of the Blind (NFB). Additional information is available on the NOPBC website (*www.nfb.org*).

It is possible for a child to be considered legally blind, have need of specialized educational materials, and yet walk independently using his residual sight and/or skills learned through orientation and mobility training. Other children who are blind use a cane or walk with a sighted person serving as a guide. Typically a guide dog is not used until the child reaches his mid to late teens.

Strabismus

Strabismus is a condition in which the eyes are not focused in the same direction. One eye may point at an angle (wandering eye), or the eyes may point inward (cross-eyed). Strabismus can often be corrected with surgery, with the use of an eye patch, or through exercises to strengthen the eye muscles.

Astigmatism

Astigmatism (often incorrectly called "stigmatism") is a condition caused by an irregularly shaped lens or cornea. Astigmatism can result in blurred vision, tired eyes, and headaches. As in any visual disorder, there are varying degrees of astigmatism. Corrective contact lenses or surgery may be the treatment for astigmatism.

Autism Spectrum Disorders

According to CDC studies, an average of one of every 150 children may have an Autism Spectrum Disorder (ASD). As the name implies, ASD represents a wide range of disorders with similar characteristics. In general, most children on the autism spectrum have difficulty with communication and social interaction. Most children with autism have a very specific range of interests and may seem to be obsessed with one or very few objects or activities. An obsession with trains is common. They may engage in repetitive movements such as spinning or flapping their arms. Many children who are autistic also have difficulty with tactile or sensory input.

Autism

A child with the severest form of *autism* will have difficulty talking about even basic things that she needs or wants. This difficulty with communication and the tendency to act impulsively impacts social behavior. Instead of asking for a drink of water, she may simply take a drink from the bottle that is sitting on a desk.

Flapping, spinning, and other repetitive movements are common with this level of autism. Repeating certain words or phrases is also typical. Some children recite certain lines (or even scenes) from a favorite movie.

Asperger Syndrome

Children with *Asperger syndrome* are able to function more successfully in academic and social situations than other children on the autism spectrum. However, children with Asperger syndrome do have very distinct special needs. They are resistant to changes in routine, including changes that involve the people in their lives, such as even a short-term absence of a parent or having a substitute teacher at school. They want things to be the same. They want items to be arranged the same way on a table or desk and furniture to remain in its usual place.

Children with Asperger syndrome have difficulty with social communication. Often they avoid eye contact. The typical give and take of conversations is difficult, and they do not pick up on the social cues of body language. They interpret things that are said very concretely. For example, the expression "to have something up your sleeve" might be interpreted as something (other than the child's arm) is indeed inside his sleeve and is cause for concern.

PDD

A child who has extreme difficulty with social conversation (the back and forth exchange of ideas and eye contact) may be diagnosed with *Pervasive Development Disorder* (PDD). A child with PDD will often have obsessive interests like other children on the autism spectrum.

Tactile Defensiveness

More and more children are diagnosed with special needs involving sensory integration dysfunction. Sensory integration is the ability to tolerate or process the input acquired from the senses.

Most children on the autism spectrum have some level of *tactile defensiveness*. For some children, touching things with unusual textures is a challenge. They may not like to touch things that are sticky (glue or certain foods) or slimy. They may not like to wash their hands. Even the tag on the back of clothing may be extremely uncomfortable for them.

When a child has extreme tactile defensiveness, combined with a need for things to be familiar, eating difficulties can result. A child with this level of oral tactile defensiveness may have only a few foods in his diet. If the child's diet does not include needed nutritional variety, other health issues can follow. Sometimes children avoid crunchy foods, which can result in dental concerns.

Behavioral Disorders

Behavioral disorders are among the most puzzling special needs. Some behaviors seem to be embedded in other special needs. (The autistic child is often obsessed with routine, and yet autism is a condition in and of itself.) Physiological, chemical, genetic, and environmental causes play a part in behaviors, but many emotional and behavioral concerns remain a mystery.

Obsessive-Compulsive Disorder (OCD)

The child who is *obsessive-compulsive* believes things *must* be done a certain way. Rituals of the child might include bathing (how long he bathes or how often he does so), eating (the arrangement of foods on the plate and the order in which they are eaten), and routines (dressing, eating breakfast, brushing teeth— *in a consistent order*). Sometimes the rituals have little impact on others and help the child stay calm and focused. Most of the time, however, the rituals become so irrational that they are disruptive to the child's functioning at school and to the day-to-day life of his family.

Oppositional Defiant Disorder (ODD)

The child who has *oppositional defiant disorder* is easily angered. It may seem that when you say "stand," your child sits. You say "yes"; he says "no." It is possible for the child with oppositional defiant disorder to work himself into an argument even when you are in agreement.

A child with oppositional defiant disorder will have difficulty in a variety of situations at school. If you question his impulsive actions in the cafeteria or on the playground, he will see little reason to have followed the rules. In the classroom, he may get upset about the requirements of an assignment (especially if there are multiple parts) and opt to do it his way.

Other Behavioral Disorders

Anxiety, depression, schizophrenia, neurosis, psychosis, bipolar disorder, conduct disorder, anorexia, and bulimia are other behavioral disorders that can affect children in every area of their lives. Consult your child's doctor or teacher for resources to meet your child's unique needs. Parenting groups are also great places to exchange ideas with families struggling with similar situations.

Learning Disabilities

The term *learning disability* is used to describe any of several conditions in which the child has trouble with schoolwork despite average (or above average) intelligence. In some capacity, the child has difficulty understanding and remembering what is explained or taught.

Memory Difficulties

Many children with learning disabilities struggle with memory. Some can remember information for short periods of time. During a series of lessons, a child might remember how to solve a particular problem. But at the end of the quarter, she may not be able to remember the skill that she seemed to have mastered earlier.

Another memory difficulty for kids with learning disabilities is an intermittent memory. Some days the child may understand what is being explained and can complete assignments with little difficulty. On other days, she seems to be hearing the information for the first time.

ADD

A child who has *attention deficit disorder* (ADD) has extreme difficulty focusing on a task. Everything (and nothing) seems to be a distraction. An eraser in her desk can become an airplane in flight, a football, a dancing person, or just something to pick apart. Even the quiet whisper sound of an air-conditioning unit can be a distraction.

ADHD

A child who has *attention deficit hyperactivity disorder* (ADHD) is easily distracted but also has a need to be on the move. This child might be standing at her desk when her classmates are sitting. She has difficulty waiting in line at school, and her impulsive actions get her in trouble.

Dyslexia

Dyslexia is a type of learning disability affecting the ability to read. A child who is dyslexic has trouble translating the letters and words she sees on a paper into sounds. Indeed, she may not see the letters or words as others see them. Although a child with dyslexia has difficulty reading, she has at least normal intelligence.

Dysgraphia

A child with *dysgraphia* has a learning disability in the area of writing. She may not be able to write in a designated space, such as on the line on a worksheet, on lined notebook paper, or in an answer box. Even making the marks to form written letters may be difficult for her and the results may look like disconnected, skewed lines.

Dyscalculia

Dyscalculia refers to a learning disability in math. A child with dyscalculia may have significant difficulty remembering basic math facts. She may not understand the concepts needed to complete math story problems or to compute problems that involve multiple steps.

CHAPTER 3

Great Expectations

You may have found out about your child's disability at her birth, or you may not have learned of it until she attended school. In either case, such news initially brings grief and questions of *why*. As you accept the needs of your child and how they will impact her life, you will come back to the great expectations that every parent shares. Sometimes the details of the expectations may vary as you help your child discover what is best for her.

Happiness

Every parent wants her child to be happy. Regardless of frustrations with understanding special needs, being an advocate for your child, and dealing with all of the common parenting concerns, the bottom line is whether or not your child is happy. This is not a happiness that involves your child having possessions or getting to do everything that she wants. This is a happiness of personal fulfillment.

Get to know your child. What are her interests? You will be better equipped to help her reach her personal goals as she gets older.

A Different Kind of Happiness

Think for a moment about the things that make you happy. What brings you personal satisfaction? You may list family, work, hobbies, friends, travel, financial freedom, or any number of things that bring joy into your life. You, no doubt, have a definition of happiness for your own life.

 Alert

If you define your child's happiness by what makes you happy or by what you hope she will do, you will be disappointed. It doesn't mean that she will not pursue meaningful activities. It does mean that they will likely be different than your ideas. This has little to do with special needs, but is about her being a separate individual.

Your child may not share your goals or definition of happiness. You may be an avid collector of antiques or a cycling enthusiast. If your child has extreme autism, however, she may love hours on a trampoline. You may thrive on hours at the mall shopping, but large crowds may be difficult for your child to tolerate. Even the noise of shoppers may be painful for a child on the autism spectrum. Perhaps you love concerts. If your child is profoundly deaf, her enjoyment of concerts will be limited unless an interpreter is available.

Redefining Happy

Think about the things that make your child happy. As with all people, it does not mean that she can (or should) do those things all day long. Having a list of happy things, though, is a wonderful way to plan rewards for good behavior or hard work, as well as just a way to relax.

Help your child explore interests and aptitudes for work and hobbies. Plan opportunities for experiences in the community and with friends. Being happy is a lifelong pursuit for all of us— including the child with special needs.

Communication

Communication through words, and reading facial expressions and body language, is how people interact. Society's goal for every child is to be able to express himself. The child with a special need will often have to learn specific skills in a sequence to accomplish this.

Expressing Wants and Needs

It is important for your child to develop communication skills to ask for things. You may feel that you know your child's thoughts and can save him frustration by giving him what he wants before it becomes a situation out of control, but this will not help your child in the longrun.

Work with your child on socially acceptable ways to ask for the things he wants and needs:

- In the beginning, have the child point to an item or a picture instead of just taking it or going into meltdown.
- Focus on a specific area (perhaps asking for a drink of water).
- Show your child how to sign or say "water please."
- Have another family member model the request and then reward that person with the requested water.
- When your child attempts to ask for water, repeat the request, and then reward him with the drink.
- Always reward attempts to request something.

Make a list of things you want your child to be able to request: food, toys, activities, choice in clothing, TV programs, DVDs, and music CDs. Work with him on the things that are most important to him first; he will be motivated to ask for them. Chances are that these are the requests that will come up most often. Gradually add other things to your list.

Questions

How frustrating it must be to not be able to ask questions! You ask questions to get information about things you don't understand. You ask questions to understand what is coming next. You ask questions just out of curiosity.

Practice questions and answers with your child. Use the pattern that you used to help him ask for things. Focus on a few types of questions and then expand to others.

Even though *why* seems to be the question that preschoolers adore, it is the last question to practice. It is by far the most difficult to understand. Start with *who* and *what*. When your child is having some success, go on to *where* and *when*.

Expressing Feelings

Use pictures and books to work with your child on expressing feelings. Talk about how the person feels. Keep your wording simple: "The girl is sad. The girl dropped her ice cream." Focus on basic feelings (happy, sad, mad, tired) and then include other feelings one at a time.

 Fact

Don't introduce new words and phrases too quickly. All children learn language spontaneously in steps. Learning language is a baby-step process for children with special needs. A typically developing baby sitting in the highchair hears mom talking about food. She picks up on the words and sentences. A baby with special needs will require more focused, direct practice.

Basic Conversations

Basic conversations are hard for many kids with special needs. Understanding how to use questions, practicing the give and take of basic conversation skills, staying on the topic of the conversation, and making eye contact can be difficult. These are skills that are often practiced with the speech and language therapist, but follow-up at home is also important.

Learning

Learning continues beyond the school years. It is a lifelong skill that allows people to adapt to changing expectations and demands of life. What the young child with special needs should learn in an early childhood classroom is very different than what she should learn to handle bills and care for an apartment. Parents should expect their children to be lifelong learners despite special needs.

Learning in Steps

Most children with special needs can learn many things. In most cases, their learning goes beyond what we imagined possible when they were infants, often just struggling for their lives. But it is necessary to structure their learning in small steps. The child with ADD or ADHD has difficulty zeroing in on the important information and ignoring everything else. The child with a hearing loss may be overwhelmed with unfamiliar words in an explanation. Start slowly, and focus on specific vocabulary, wording, or instructions in small steps.

Learning with Peers

Children want to be a part of "the group." They want to be accepted. Parents have the same goals for their children—socially and in the area of learning. You will need to work with the staff at your child's school to figure out just what that means. One part of the goal is to work out a schedule that allows your child to be in the inclusion classroom for as much instruction and as many activities as possible. Equally important is for your child to be in an appropriate learning environment. The challenge is creating a schedule that meets her individual needs: academic readiness, resiliency in transitions, and stamina.

Some children with special needs can function in the inclusion classroom with little or no assistance. Some have only modifications and accommodations outlined in a 504 plan. Other children, however, need special instruction to learn without frustration. Often, this is in the special education classroom.

Expect your child to learn to her highest ability. Plan to give her the necessary services and support to meet that goal. Remember that her ideal learning environment for all instruction may, or may not, be in the inclusion room. The important thing is to assist her in growing and learning.

True Understanding

Remember cramming for a test and forgetting the information by the next day? If a child with special needs crams for a test, she may learn the right things to say and how to approach written work that makes it look like she understands—and yet she does not.

So how can you tell if your child truly understands? If she is in the early grades, have her retell what she has read. In the upper grades, have her summarize the information in her own words. Don't rely on the age-old question: "Do you understand?" You will almost always get a yes answer. No one wants to admit a lack of understanding.

Behavior

Expect great behavior from your child. For a child with special needs, you may need to adapt how you communicate your behavioral expectations. The guidelines and consequences will need to be especially clear and consistent for a child with a behavior disorder, hyperactivity, or impulsive behavior. A special need does not mean that a child has an excuse to act inappropriately.

Set Rules

You will need to decide on the rules. This sounds obvious, but too often parents have not thoroughly thought through their expectations. Even worse, they may not have come to an agreement between themselves on just what those expectations are.

Prioritize the rules you want your child to follow. He may not be able to understand a complex set of table manners, but he will understand the rule for saying "please" and "thank you," and for clearing his own plate if you set the expectation. Once you have the basics, you can build on them.

Following and Understanding Rules

Sometimes following and understanding rules are two different things. This is similar to understanding *why* questions. Strive to have your child follow rules first. Then use pictures and straightforward explanation to help him increase understanding as his language skills develop. Be aware that some kids with special needs have a lot of trouble visualizing consequences of their actions: *I won't run on the wet pool deck because I might fall.*

Age-Appropriate Behavior

Understand age-appropriate behavior. It is easy to focus on the progress your child is making and to lose sight of what other children his age are doing. He may love anything with an action figure design on it, but that may not be what most sixth graders are carrying on their lunchboxes. Help him choose a box with a design that might remind him of the action figure, but will look more age-appropriate.

Social Behavior

Help your child develop appropriate social behavior by establishing some basic dos and don'ts. A child with Down syndrome may not be ready to understand the behavior nuances for a boy-girl get-together, but he can understand that he should not hug every friend.

Life Skills

Some adults with special needs lead perfectly independent lives, are leaders in the community, and earn a very nice income. Others will need some assistance to get along as adults. This, of course, depends on the individual and her needs. Don't let anyone steer your thoughts toward the limits of your child. Yes, you should be practical and realize when your child has reached her potential in an area, but you should never stop being her encourager and advocate.

Self-Care

Having routine times for bathing, brushing teeth, and so on will help your child develop good self-care habits. Every member of your family practices self-care, so enlist them as role models. Ask siblings to wash their hands together before a meal. Have them brush their teeth at the same time before bed. Take your child with you for mother-daughter haircut appointments.

Household Skills

Develop the same kinds of routines with household chores. Most children with special needs can be involved in jobs around the house. A child with a severe physical disability might be in charge of starting a favorite family music CD to keep everyone going, or watching the clock to announce break times.

Many special needs have little effect on the ability to complete household chores. A child with ADHD can load the dishwasher and a teen with a learning disability can mow the grass. Expect that your child will be a "working" member of your family.

Financial Concerns

As you would with your other children, teach money skills starting at an early age. Increase the skill expectation as your child gets older and is mature enough to handle new concepts. For example:

- Teach your child to recognize the individual values of coins and paper money.
- Have her earn an allowance by completing family jobs.
- Let her practice counting money and checking her change when she buys garage sale treasures or small items at a store.
- Have her save for a desired item or activity.
- When she is old enough, let her run errands for you to pick up bread, milk, or eggs.
- Help her establish a checking and savings account.
- Work with her to make simple purchases and pay small bills using her accounts.

Not every child will become financially independent, but routine money practice will establish sound habits for any living arrangement in the future.

Living Independently

All of the topic discussions in this chapter lead up to the question: "Will my child be able to live on her own?" The answers vary as much as each child and teen. For some, living alone is possible. Others will need the support of a sheltered living facility or group home. Many of these homes have live-in helpers for transportation and to serve as a resource when needed.

Role Models with Disabilities

Children look up to their parents. Parents have the daunting task of being a child's first and main teachers throughout life. There is a point, however, when every child looks outside the home to peers and others in the world as role models. For the child with a disability, having role models with similar struggles is encouraging. It says: "You can do it!"

Peers

Get to know your child's classmates. Which ones are using strategies to compensate for their special needs? Which ones are good influences? Which ones are just plain nice kids? Chances are that these kids and their families will become your friends. You can help each other navigate the waters of new expectations as your children grow.

Community Members

Check out adult members of the community with special needs who might be a part of a social club or support agency. Get involved in activities with these role models and with your child.

Adults with disabilities can help you better understand what your child is feeling. Volunteers in support agencies sometimes are parents of special needs children (or adults). They, too, can offer guidance in home, community, and school situations. Sometimes, they can serve as advocates for you and your child.

 Fact

Sometimes, if a child with a special need never interacts with adults having the same disability, they logically assume that they will outgrow the disability. Often deaf children who are not around deaf adults assume that they will hear when they grow up. Look for and help your child get to know role models with similar disabilities.

Famous Faces of Special Needs

Look to famous faces for role models for your child. This is an age of disability awareness, and prominent people with special needs can be found in every area of the media and throughout the pages of history books. TV and sport stars as well as popular entertainers with disabilities can be an inspiration.

Check websites of organizations that focus on your child's specific needs to find information about celebrities and historical figures with disabilities. Spread the word about famous individuals who have beat the odds.

Famous Faces Without Names

Sometimes the famous faces of disability awareness do not come with a name. Do an Internet search for posters, T-shirts, mugs, and toys that portray awareness of your child's needs. They make great gifts for teachers, coaches, child care providers, family, and friends. After all, the more that people are aware of the needs of people with disabilities, the better the quality of life will be for all.

Check with your library for information on children's books about specific disabilities. (Refer to the NICHCY resource link in Appendix A.) Sharing books with your child and his friends will promote awareness and acceptance.

Groups and Gatherings

The minute your child was born she became a part of many groups: family, neighborhood, community, newborn peers, and babies with special needs. Expect that your child will become an active member of those groups. Expect that the people in these groups will accept and nurture your child as an individual with gifts, strengths, weaknesses, and needs.

Family and Friends

You should expect that your family and friends will be involved in your life and the life of your baby. The birth of a baby with special needs does not change your need for contact with others. In fact, it increases that need. Sadly, in a few situations, parents are not always around to see their children grow up. Taken by illness or injury, the loss of a parent calls for family or friends to step in. That transition, if necessary, will be easier for all if they are involved in your child's life from the beginning.

Peers

Expect that your child will be connected with her peers (disabled and nondisabled). A child with special needs should not live a sheltered life away from others. Peers force us to grow and catch us when we fall. Peers are the lifelong travelers with us on earth. Expect your child to be involved with her peers throughout her life.

Community Activities

Anticipate that you will need a little time to come to grips with how to help your child. Most parents did not expect to have a child with special needs. They are overwhelmed with appointments and things that need to be done—including a time of grief.

Give yourself some space and some time. Then jump back into the swing of things. You may need to tweak your involvement in community activities, but do not pull out of everything you were involved in before your baby's birth. Community activities will be important for your child's development and your own personal satisfaction. Plan to stay involved.

Agencies for Special Needs

At first, you will be dealing with appointments and questions, and will be working to meet the physical needs of your baby. Soon you will be looking for others who are on a similar path. Become involved with community agencies that work with families of children with special needs. Get involved early. Involve your child. Community agencies with years of experience are there to help.

Contribution to Society

Parents dream that their children will work to benefit society. While every parent may not anticipate raising a doctor or lawyer, the desire for the child to contribute to society is strong. Children with special needs may make a difference in many ways and to many people, including:

- **Family:** Parents of children with Down syndrome know the compassion their child has for others. Smiles and hugs are freely given. A child with Down syndrome continually reminds his family and everyone around him that compassion is an important character trait. And he can make this understood without ever speaking a word.
- **Peers:** A child with cerebral palsy may work hard to walk and to accomplish small self-care tasks like buttoning his clothes or feeding himself. He is often the self-declared cheerleader for his peers. His can-do attitude can encourage others to keep trying.
- **Community:** In community activities, a teen with a disability strives to be a team player. He is anxious to pitch in where he can make a difference. His motivation and cooperation encourage others to do the same.
- **Job:** Any person can have a vast range of jobs. Some individuals with special needs are prominent on TV and in sports. Others have more commonplace jobs alongside their non-disabled peers in an office.

Does everyone with a special need have a positive, encouraging attitude toward the world? Of course not, but most respond to the challenges they have overcome in a way that is inspiring to others.

Quality of Life

The quality of your child's life does not depend on the nature of her disability or what she can and cannot do. The quality of her life will largely depend on her attitude (and yours) toward struggles and choices that come her way.

Relationships

Some people will be helpful, and some will be too helpful. Teach your child that not all people have the same approach to someone with special needs. Help her develop friendships where others see her as a person first, not a "disabled person." Help her to seek and develop the friendships that encourage, support, and challenge her to reach her potential.

Recreation and Hobbies

Help your child explore recreation and hobbies that are relaxing and enjoyable. Find some things that you can enjoy together to strengthen your parent-child bond. Allow her to add activities based on her own interests. Expect that your child will have unique ideas to explore and enjoy.

Independence

A child with special needs is dependent on others for so many things. She may need physical assistance. For some children, everyday tasks like homework and household chores may require redirection and supervision. Seek the ways that your child can be independent. If her homework requires that she write spelling words and complete math story problems, for example, decide what she can do independently. Chances are she can write the spelling words without someone sitting with her. Use that opportunity to start supper or read to another child. Expect that she will do some things independently, and offer praise when she does.

Self-Worth

Quality of life largely depends on a child's perception of herself, her circumstances, her struggles, and her accomplishments. No one is supposed to be good at everything. *Everyone* is good at some things. Expect that your child will develop a healthy self-concept. Lead the way with your own realistic encouragement and acceptance.

CHAPTER 4

Medical Concerns

Medical decisions (medications, procedures and surgeries, and medical equipment) can be a large part of the responsibility of parents with a child who has special needs. The purpose of this chapter (and of this book) is not to influence medical decisions or to make medical recommendations. Rather, it is intended to offer some questions that may be useful for discussion with your child's doctor. Only you and your doctor can make appropriate medical decisions for your child.

Choosing a Pediatrician

Depending on his special needs, your child will likely have a pediatrician and one or more specialists. Perhaps he will see the pediatrician more often than the specialists. Having a pediatrician who is a good match for the job is important; you need an individual with the right kind of training and experience.

Talk to the Doctor

Consult the doctor regarding his comfort level and his experience with your child's specific conditions. He may be the long-time family doctor, and you may want to maintain that relationship. However, prescribing an antibiotic for an older sister's sore throat is not the same as recognizing congenital heart defect complications. You will have specialists treat involved conditions, but you want your pediatrician to make appropriate recommendations for your child's general care and to recognize red flags.

 Fact

The American Academy of Pediatrics (*www.aap.org*) provides an on-line referral service to help you find doctors. When using this free service, you can indicate a geographic area as well as the medical specialty that is needed.

If you decide to choose a physician other than your family doctor, it does not mean that all of your children must change doctors. In fact, some specialized pediatricians only see children with extreme medical conditions and needs.

Talk to Other Parents

Other parents you may have met from your experience in the neonatal intensive care unit (NICU), and those you meet from your child's school program and disability-related organizations can be a valuable resource of information about physicians. Questions you'll want to ask of other parents or a physician's office staff include:

- What is the physician's specialty?
- How quickly are calls returned?
- Is he accepting new patients?
- Are other physicians in the practice?
- What insurance is accepted by the practice?
- What are the hours and location of the physician's office?
- Which hospital(s) does the physician serve?
- How well does the physician interact with the child?

- Is he in that office every weekday or is his time split with an office in another location?
- Do parents feel comfortable asking for additional information?

 Essential

Your child's pediatrician and any specialists should have privileges at the same hospital. If your child is hospitalized, it will be much easier to coordinate care with familiar physicians. It will also be easier for the doctors to have timely access to needed reports and to consult with each other.

Keep an objective approach as you are gathering information. It's possible for a family to have a negative experience with any doctor. It does not necessarily mean that you should mark that doctor off the list to be considered. However, if you hear consistently negative reports from several families, that particular physician may not be for you.

Research Your Options

Spend some time researching on the Internet and on the phone. You will not want to choose a physician based on an advertisement in the telephone book, but it can give you a place to start. You will gain a lot of insight about a medical practice by the way the physician and his staff respond to your questions. Remember, you are searching for a physician who is experienced in treating children with special needs. Their willingness to take time to answer your questions is important to making your decision. Consider asking for a consultative appointment to see if the physician is a good match for your family's communication and information needs, as well as for the medical needs of your child.

Medication

To medicate or not to medicate? At some point in your child's life you will likely have that decision to make. Some children are prescribed medications because of serious medical conditions such as epilepsy or diabetes. Obviously, these children must have prescribed medication. Often it is necessary for survival.

For other children the decision might not be as clear cut. Some children may be considered for medication because of behavioral or attention disorders that are most apparent in quiet, work settings like school. The considerations vary from child to child. Some parents prefer for their child not to be on medication at all.

If your child is "on meds," have a plan that includes a paperwork safety net to administer them. Perhaps the parents' work schedules mean that it is not always the same parent giving the medication. Have a chart that is kept near the medication, and away from the reach of children. Record each date and time the medication is given.

With some attention deficit medications, parents choose not to medicate their child in the evenings, on weekends, and other times when the child is not attending school. Consideration should be given to the impact on the child's ability to complete school assignments as well as to participate in extracurricular activities. If you are discussing medication with your child's doctor, you may want to use some of the questions in Chapter 11 to get an idea of the best choice for your child. Only you and your doctor can make that decision.

Specialists

Parents of kids with special needs have so many decisions—just in the medical arena alone. Most likely your child will see medical specialists. You may have inherited some from your baby's experience in the NICU. You also may be looking for one because of a newly diagnosed condition.

Your child might see one or more specialists to meet his unique needs. For example, a child with ADHD might see one of several professionals. According to the National Institute of Mental Health website (*www.nimh.nih.gov*), some common specialists for children with ADHD include:

- Child psychiatrist
- Psychologist
- Developmental/behavioral pediatrician
- Behavioral neurologist
- Clinical social worker

Although all of these professionals are familiar with ADHD, the psychologist and the clinical social worker cannot diagnose it or prescribe medication.

 **Alert**

Verify that the physician's office accepts your medical insurance. Find out if the insurance company or the doctor's office requires a referral before services can be offered. Usually the front desk will ask about this information when you make your first appointment.

When looking for a specialist, consider the suggestions for finding a pediatrician. In a specialist, you are looking for experience, although a new physician may have had wonderful internship experience. The experience should be centered on the special need and in children. For example, a physician who treats adults for arthritis may not be the best choice to treat a child with juvenile arthritis.

Think about whether or not the specialists are on the same hospital staff. If one recommends the other, they are likely a team, accustomed to working together on decisions and procedures that require the expertise of both fields. While being on the same staff is not always necessary, it often eases the coordination of services and access of records. Ask lots of questions. You are looking to be on the team that serves your child. It is important to have a good *working* relationship with all of your child's doctors from the beginning.

Therapy Is Prescribed by Specialists

Therapy goes hand in hand with medical treatment. Most children with special needs will see some kind of therapist more often than they see a doctor. For some children, it might only be a speech therapist at school. For others, the therapist list is long and may include school personnel as well as professionals in the community.

If you are looking for a therapist in the community, begin by consulting your child's specialists. Very often, they will have particular therapists who handle their referrals. Sometimes they are even housed in the same suite of offices. If you are pleased with the specialist, you will most likely be pleased with his referral. Here is a summary of benefits to using this referral system:

- Location
- Communication between offices (reports, consultations)
- Understanding of the other professional's manner of work
- Some ease in your own paperwork
- Possible insurance paperwork convenience

For more information about specific kinds of therapy (physical, occupational, vision, speech and language), see Chapter 6. The basic information about therapies and the required doctor prescriptions apply to any age.

Hospitals

Most children with special needs are not complete strangers to hospitals. Fragile medical conditions, illness, accident, and surgery can cause a child to be hospitalized. Know which hospital can best serve your child well in advance of needing its services. In many situations, families will have one hospital preference for planned procedures and a closer-to-home option for emergencies.

Find a Hospital

Like finding a doctor or a therapist, you will want a hospital that understands children and particularly children with special needs. Depending on your child's medical needs, you may be searching for a hospital that specializes even further, perhaps in the area of orthopedic or cardiac services.

The National Association of Children's Hospitals and Related Institutions website (*www.childrenshospitals.net*) has a search form to locate specialized children's hospitals. A search can be entered by area of specialization and by geographic area. The website also can be used to find camps, day care, dentists, and current research.

Most large metropolitan areas have a children's hospital. There are several hospitals that draw children nationwide and sometimes worldwide. Currently, there are twenty-two Shriners Hospitals for Children around the world. These hospitals specialize in orthopedics, burn care, spinal cord injury, and cleft lip and palate care. All care provided at a Shriners Hospital is free of charge to the family.

 Fact

Many large hospitals have a nearby place of calm and caring for families. Ronald McDonald Houses are located throughout the world. They offer free lodging, meals, and a place for children to attend school away from home. Each family's room is decorated with a child-friendly theme. Families who stay there find care and support from other families as well as from volunteers.

Located in Memphis, Tennessee, the St. Jude Children's Research Hospital focuses on pediatric cancer and other serious illnesses. According to the hospital's website (*www.stjude.org*), fundraising covers the cost of any authorized treatment at St. Jude Children's Research Hospital not paid by insurance or Medicaid.

Emergency Care

Prevention, practice, and *paper preparation* are the key words for emergency care for a child with special needs. *Prevention* begins by making sure your house is as safe for your child as possible. Keep harmful substances out of reach. A child with cognitive delays is more at risk of ingesting a harmful substance than other children. Cleaners, medications, alcohol, bottles of soap, lighter fluids, and pet products are a few possible dangers. However, some children will sample the unlikely. A child with Down syndrome may get into the fireplace, playing in the ashes and tasting them. A child who is severely autistic may play with and sample his own feces.

Also make sure that other kinds of dangerous items are out of reach as well. These items can include knives, matches, lighters, ice picks, scissors, rotary cutters, and tools. Talk with your family and child care providers about dangerous items and dangerous situations for your child. A child with a hearing loss may not know that someone is calling for him to stop at a busy street. A child who has ADHD may impulsively climb too high on playground equipment.

A medical emergency is always a possibility—even with the best care. So give your child opportunities to *practice* medical emergencies. Use a doll or stuffed animal as the model at home. Seeing a cherished toy being cared for will show your child that the emergency medical care provider is to be trusted, although it may be scary at the time.

Plan outings to visit fire departments, EMT stations, hospitals, and medical offices when they offer open houses. Take the trusted doll or stuffed animal along and let it sit in the treatment chair or lie on the bed. Also have a sibling or parent try it out. Encourage your child to do the same.

Paper preparation will help when a medical emergency does arrive. Maintain an updated medical information sheet. The *Emergency Information Form for Children with Special Health Care Needs* is recommended by the American College of Emergency Physicians and the American Academy of Pediatrics and can be downloaded at *www .acep.org*. Use the form for the doctor's office, emergency room, and when assisted by EMTs. Keep one copy in your purse, in the insurance notebook (See section at the end of this chapter), in an accessible location at home, at school, and with your family's child care provider.

Dental Care

Dental care is another medical concern for many families. Opposition to basic dental hygiene, limited diet, physical disability, sensory issues, and resistance to professional dental care can be obstacles to keeping those pearly whites in good shape.

Prevention

Healthy dental care habits can be tricky to instill in a child with special needs. If your child is able to brush his own teeth, try to establish a routine at a very young age. (See Chapter 17.) Your child may respond to brushing with a sibling. Children are powerful role models for other children. Chances are that your child wants to be like his siblings. Establish a tooth brushing routine for everyone . . . together.

Contributions to Unhealthy Teeth

Some children do not have proper eating habits to maintain strong healthy teeth. This could be the result of a physical disability that prevents the child from chewing hard, crunchy foods.

A diet limited by sensory issues can also have a detrimental effect on dental health. Some children with autism will eat only a few preferred foods. They may never eat crunchy carrots or apples. They may never use their teeth to bite and chew a piece of meat. With time, the teeth can become soft and more susceptible to decay.

Fact

Some conditions necessitate seeing a dentist experienced with special needs. Severe malformations of the teeth and oral cavity can cause treatment complications. In the case of a child with fibrodysplasia ossificans progressiva (FOP), there is a risk of the jaw remaining open permanently after dental procedures are completed.

Professional Dental Care

When it comes time to visit the dental hygienist or dentist, there are additional concerns. Sometimes it is difficult to find a dentist who will treat a child with special needs. The dentist's reluctance could come from several reasons:

- Lack of training
- Lack of proper equipment
- Lack of understanding of special needs
- Fear of unintentionally hurting the child
- Insufficient time to make treatment cost effective

Use the National Association of Children's Hospitals and Related Institutions website to find a dentist who has experience in treating children with special needs (*www.childrenshospitals.net*).

Whether your child will see your family dentist, a pediatric dentist, or a dentist who is experienced in treating children with special needs, you will want to practice with your child before he goes to the dentist's office. Use the same technique as when practicing for a medical emergency. (See the discussion of emergency care earlier.) Have a doll or stuffed animal be the first dental patient. Then a sibling or parent can be the patient while someone else is the dentist. Be sure to encourage your child to take a turn at the mock dentist's office as well.

Another way to practice is to use a children's book about visiting the dentist. You may read the text or have your child read it depending on his cognitive and language skills. The most important thing is to talk about the pictures. Then talk about your child being the one who will go to see the dentist.

Insurance

The medical side of a special need can mean big medical bills. The cost of surgeries and outpatient procedures, therapies, medications, and specialized equipment adds up quickly. Every family needs health insurance, and it becomes a more extreme need for the family with a child with special needs.

Private Health Insurance

Insurance is gold to the family trying to keep up with an avalanche of medical bills. Having two insurance providers is great. Having high-paying plans is even better. However, parents of the child with special needs often find that the decision for both parents to work is complicated due to child care.

Government Supported Health Insurance

Some children may be eligible for a government medical insurance program such as Medicaid. Parents' income cannot disqualify a child from being eligible, but there are other factors that come into play. You must first apply for Medicaid in order for your child's eligibility to be considered. Only a qualified caseworker can help you determine if your child qualifies.

Children of working families who do not qualify for Medicaid may be eligible for the State Children's Health Insurance Program (SCHIP). This program (offered in every state) offers free or low-cost health insurance for basic medical care. The Centers for Medicare and Medicaid website (*www.cms.hhs.gov*) lists doctor visits, immunizations, hospitalizations, and emergency room visits as services covered under SCHIP.

Organize Medical Treatment Documents

Create an insurance notebook to keep track of all of your paperwork. You will need the following supplies:

- Sturdy three-ring binder, three inches thick
- Dividers (one for your insurance company information and one for each provider)
- Three-hole punch
- Notebook paper
- Notebook-sized calendar
- Pencils or erasable pens

Setting up an insurance notebook is easy. Following through and using it is the trick. Make sure you have copies of your insurance cards and policies in the front of the notebook. Then add some lined paper to the front of each section so you can document your child's office visits and any contact you have with that office or with the insurance company. Remember to put the date at the beginning of each entry.

As you receive reports or billing statements, place them in the correct section with the most recent ones in front. If you have two insurance providers, you will need to keep statements from both companies together for tracking payments from each company made on the same bill. Having all of the medical billing information in one place will help you locate information when you are paying bills, calling for clarification, or verifying that all claims have been processed.

CHAPTER 5

Parents Are People Too

P eople often say that the birth of a child will change your life for-ever. It's especially true if your child has a special need. One thing that does not change is the fact that you have basic needs as a person. If you spend all of your time and effort meeting the needs of your child, soon you will be without energy and ideas. Plan to take care of your own needs so that you can be a better parent to your child.

Give Yourself a Break

It is critical to be kind to yourself. You will be dealing with feelings of disappointment and guilt, or that you are being punished for your actions. The truth is that having a child with a special need does not happen as a punishment. Parents do not have a baby with a disability because they are bad people.

Parents often worry that they could have prevented their baby's disability. Despite their reading books and magazines and following advice about diet and other critical issues of pregnancy, things can go wrong. Sometimes parents blame each other. It is natural to feel responsible, but most often there is nothing that could have been done differently. Some disabilities are the result of complications during pregnancy or birth. Some happen for unknown reasons. You may need to forgive yourself and your spouse—even though there is nothing really to forgive.

In a small percentage of cases, a disability happens because of genetic conditions unknown to the parents. Talk with your doctor about the possible causes of your baby's condition. Seek his advice or the advice of a doctor who specializes in genetic counseling to see if there is a similar risk with future children.

Seek the facts about your child's condition. Talk about your feelings with your spouse, and take time to heal. Try to accept that life is often unfair, and turn your combined efforts toward your baby. She will need both of you to get along and reach her highest potential.

Child Care

You will at some point need child care. Perhaps you work outside of your home or are a student. Perhaps you just need someone to watch your child so you can get the groceries or to be available in case of an emergency that calls you away.

Types of Child Care

Providing child care for the child with special needs involves more than finding a dependable person or place that charges reasonable rates. You will need to make sure the unique requirements of your child can be met. You must make sure that the therapists who work with your child have access to your child when she is not at home. You will need to coordinate with those therapists for ways you can keep up on the skills your child should practice.

It may seem overwhelming to set up childcare for the child with special needs. There are options to make it more workable:

- Consider child care provided by a relative, family friend, or nanny who can come into your home.
- Check into day cares that will include your child with children who do not have special needs.
- Check with local agencies and your parent-infant educator for specialized day care programs in your area.

Most children with special needs will enter an early childhood education program in a school setting at age three. Besides providing important instruction and therapy, this time can be used by parents for work, errands, and fulfilling responsibilities to other family members.

Info for Child Care Providers

It is critical that your child care providers (even a relative or the teenager from down the street) have adequate information to care for your child. They don't have to know every detail of your child's history, much of which may be personal. But they do need to know about communication and medical details to keep your child safe. Following is a basic checklist of important information to give all your child care providers:

CHILD CARE PROVIDER CHECKLIST

✓ Phone numbers for both parents
✓ Doctor's phone number
✓ Phone number for relative who is familiar with the needs, preferences of the child
✓ Emergency numbers: ambulance, fire, police
✓ Medication information (including times and amounts)
✓ Allergies (if applicable)
✓ Child's routine (meals, bedtime)
✓ Food preferences
✓ Child's communication
✓ Rules and appropriate consequences
✓ Calming techniques

Create this checklist in a form that you can use over and over. Check the information periodically and revise as needed.

At home, make sure your child care provider is aware that the checklist is near a phone. This is an especially good reminder for frequent providers who may be comfortable with your child and forget that there are important instructions in case of an emergency.

Fact

A child who is developmentally delayed may do things that seem defiant or purposefully troublesome, when it is actually a reflection of his disability. The severely autistic child who likes to bang pots and pans, for example, may empty a cupboard without close supervision. Talk to your child care provider about the behaviors and communication needs of your child.

Little Breaks

No parent can be on call twenty-four hours a day, seven days a week. It is not healthy for the parent, *and* it is not healthy for the child. While you know your baby better than anyone else, you need some breaks to recharge your energy and sometimes to re-evaluate how to best approach challenges. Make a plan so that you have the little breaks that you need.

A Schedule That Works

It's possible to plan a realistic schedule that includes time for breaks. Think about the things that have to happen: meals, baths, relaxation, sleep, housework, necessary appointments, etc. Create a schedule with time for the necessary things. Keep your child's physical needs and stamina in mind as you plan. Look for the times in the schedule that your child will be resting or away from home. Use some of this time for your breaks. Taking a needed break is much more important than adding another task to your schedule.

Schooltime

Because early childhood programs (special education for preschoolers) begin at age three, school time is an especially important break time. Plan your appointments, part-time work, and errands during this time. Even with a packed schedule (the days go quickly), schedule a little break for yourself. If might mean fifteen minutes at a park with a cup of coffee before you head off to work . . . Do it! You need a break like everyone else.

Parent Tradeoffs

Parents need two kinds of breaks. They need breaks together to stay close and plan for the future. They also need breaks individually. Parent tradeoffs are one way to set up little breaks from the responsibility of all of the children.

If you are the parent on break, make sure you are taking a break for yourself and not just rushing to get things done for the family. You could:

- Read a book.
- Take a nap.
- Chat on the phone or the Internet.
- Take a walk.
- Have a cup of coffee and do nothing.
- Enjoy a hobby.
- Shop.
- Go to lunch with your friends.

Parent tradeoff breaks can happen while one parent is on kitchen detail or watching a movie with the kids. It can happen for a longer period of time such as a whole evening or weekend.

 Alert

It is important for both parents to have breaks. If you are a stay-at-home parent, you may be waiting at the door for your break when your spouse arrives home. Remember that your spouse needs breaks, too.

Remember that you can even take a break in another room of the house. Work with your spouse and your children to respect the time that you need. It is a healthy habit for them to learn from you.

Friends and Family

Friends and family can offer small breaks. Sometimes, they might be the child care providers for you when you are not at home. They can provide the same in-house breaks for you that your spouse does. If there is a dire need for you, then you are under the same roof. Chances are, though, that everyone will get along just fine.

Helping Hands

Besides needing breaks, you will need helping hands at times. Doctors and therapy appointments, and the extra physical care and supervision your child needs, can add up to a very busy schedule. Parenting in general is a busy calling. Add on the extra demands of raising a child with special needs and time may seem to vanish. Look for those with helping hands to make it work. People who are close to you want to help; they may need a little guidance to know how.

Help with Your Child

Children do not grow up in isolation. As the parent of a child with a special need, you may have to make sure that she has opportunities to spend time with others.

Grandparents, aunts and uncles, and friends are often anxious to be involved. Sometimes they might help by practicing therapy skills. Sometimes they might offer supervision or care while you tend to other responsibilities.

Help with Your Other Children

If you have other children, you can attest to the fact that they have continuing needs despite the special needs of their sibling.

Be open to others helping with carpools. The neighborhood teen who loves to play ball can be a great practice coach. The retired neighbor may not mind reading and rereading books with your preschooler.

Household Help

This is a team effort. Talk with your spouse and children about the housework. Extra child responsibilities can mean you have less time for housecleaning, but the whole family does live there—right? Set up a plan for everyone to pitch in. If it is possible, consider paid help to come in periodically to help you cover all of the bases.

Errands

Make sure all of your errands are really necessary. For the must-go-to places, be willing to say yes when someone offers to go for you. Who cares if it is not the kind of bread you buy. Bread only lasts for a few days!

If you are running the errands, plan a route so that you can get the most done at one time. Be aware of those helping hands at pharmacy drive-throughs and errands that can be done online from home.

Listening Ears

Frustrations, worries, disappointments, and loneliness send people searching for someone to listen, as do the good things like accomplishments, good reports, and fun plans. Any parent of a two-year-old can tell you that she needs to talk about something other than puppies, dolls, and more juice. Any parent of a child who is struggling just to catch up with his peers needs to talk. It is important to have people to talk with in good times, bad times, and those everyday times when you just need to talk to another adult. Establish a network of trustworthy, compassionate people to talk with.

Family and Friends

Your family and friends may have been your sounding boards before your child was born. No doubt they still care and should be included in your group of people who will listen. Consider their advice, but remember that they are not walking in your shoes.

Other Parents

Sometimes you will need to talk to parents who are going through similar situations with their children. You may find parents in your child's school program or meet others in doctor or therapy waiting rooms. Your community may have social activities for children with special needs where you will meet even more parents.

Support Groups

Some community agencies, schools, and hospitals have parent support groups. Often support groups are led by other parents or counselors trained in working with children with special needs.

Don't forget to check for sibling groups as well. Having a sibling with special needs presents additional questions and concerns for a child. Some may be very protective of their sibling. Others may be jealous of Mom and Dad's time. Still others may be unsure what to say when talking to their peers.

Professionals

In addition to listening, professionals can offer ideas and information on available resources. Talking to a professional who works with your child can be especially helpful because that person knows your child, his history, and what does and does not work with him. Your conversations with your child's teacher, counselor, therapist, or doctor will be confidential.

Careers

Perhaps you and your spouse both worked prior to the birth of your baby. Now, like every family when a baby is born, you must make some career decisions. The decisions are more complicated when the baby has special needs.

There are lots of things to juggle when you work and have a baby with special needs. Your baby may need additional physical care, such as specialized feeding techniques, breathing treatments, or medications. You may have physical therapy exercises or language activities to practice between therapy sessions. Then there are doctor appointments—all of this in addition to cooking, cleaning, and errands outside of work.

 Question

Is it possible to work with a baby who has special needs?
Many families are able to set up a plan that allows both parents to work. Some choose to continue their current career while others opt to work part-time. Some start a home-based business. Talk with your spouse about ways your work commitments may or may not fit the needs of your family.

Money may be a consideration in your decision whether to continue working. Equipment and therapies may not be covered by insurance. You may be the spouse who carries the family insurance.

Child care for the child with special needs requires even more consideration than care for the "typically" developing siblings. Check to make sure your day care provider can offer adequate supervision and care for your child. Be sure that therapists can visit the day care center for your child's treatments. Traditional child care centers offer valuable contact with peers, but home-based care often meets the extraordinary needs of some children.

Personal Career Goals

The arrival of a baby affords you an opportunity to reconsider your personal goals and your family's needs. How can you best meet the needs of your child and your family as well as your long-range career goals? Is this a good time to take a break or does it make more sense to set up a practical family plan and to keep on working? It is a decision that only you can make.

Hobbies

A hobby provides interesting and enjoyable diversion from everyday responsibilities. Having a hobby is a great way to be good to yourself as you travel the path of parenting. If you do not have a hobby, think about something that you have always wanted to do. Many hobbies cost nothing, but the benefits are valuable.

A Break at Home

Perhaps your child has an early bedtime schedule. You have made the effort to stick to the schedule and the child is accustomed to it. Not only does the schedule work great for your child, the schedule offers you an opportunity to take a break at home— with your hobby.

Many hobbies are done at home (scrapbooking, stamping, collections, art, music), and yet they seem to take the hobbyist to another world. They provide a mental break while you are still available if your child needs you.

Physical Release

Some hobbies offer the added benefit of physical exercise. Running, biking, skiing, exercise and dance classes, sports, swimming, and plain old walking are physical hobbies that can easily fit into your schedule. Regular physical exercise is a contributing factor to strong emotional health. Exercise relieves stress and makes it easier to take a positive approach to frustrating challenges. It also promotes good physical health. As a healthier parent, you will be better able to meet your child's needs. You owe it to yourself and to your baby to exercise on a regular basis. Plan to participate in some physical exercise several times a week.

Hobbies That Make Money

Sometimes parents make a hobby into a small business. You may sell home party items, give classes, or create crafts to sell by combining a hobby and business. One key to making this kind of plan successful is to keep your expectations realistic. Be realistic about the amount of time you can devote to it, and be realistic about the amount of money you expect to make. Remember that the goal is to have a hobby to enjoy, not to get rich.

Respite Care

Respite care provides temporary relief for caregivers. It could be an after-school program for kids with special needs that allows parents to work. Respite care is often offered so that parents can take a break—perhaps to go out for the evening.

 Alert

Respite care may be offered by individuals or by organizations such as The Arc, Easter Seals, and United Cerebral Palsy. For information on respite care in your state visit the ARCH National Respite Network website (http://chtop.org/ARCH.html).

Sometimes respite care is offered for a block of time—perhaps you need to travel to care for a family member. Finding appropriate child care might be difficult. Staying at a respite care home or facility could be an option.

According to the National Resource Center for CBCAP (Community Based Child Abuse and Neglect Prevention Grants) there are several models for respite care:

- In-home respite care
- Respite care at a school, hospital, agency, or in a provider's home
- Respite care offered as a special event by the organizations on page 62
- Camps, after-school programs, and other recreational programs

Some families qualify for respite care vouchers through Medicaid or government programs. The vouchers enable the family to choose the respite care option and provider they desire. Sometimes families choose an agency's services. Other families choose an individual who may already know the child or who could be appropriately trained. The individual may offer respite care in her own home or in the child's home as both parties agree.

 Essential

Have an emergency care plan for your child. Emergencies do not give you warning so that you can make child care arrangements. If possible, acquaint your child with the person who will provide the child care. It will make it easier on both of you should the unexpected arise.

In 2006, the Lifespan Respite Care Act was passed to make respite services accessible to more families. In model programs, care is now available regardless of the age or disability of the individual.

CHAPTER 6

Help for Infants and Toddlers

Once a special need has been identified, seek services that will help your baby develop to his fullest potential. Sometimes families think that because the child is still a baby, they should only focus on love and physical care. They believe that learning activities can wait until later when the child starts school. In order for your child to do his best, it is essential to provide developmental support as well as love. The first few months and years of your baby's life are very important to his future development.

Therapy

Therapy is one kind of early education for the baby with special needs, and will usually continue through much of the child's school career as well. There are several kinds of therapy, and some babies will need more than one kind. The kind your baby should have depends on her unique needs.

A doctor or other specialized professional conducts an evaluation or test before therapy begins. For example, a baby with a suspected hearing loss is evaluated first by a doctor to rule out infection, then by an audiologist. A baby with a hearing loss would be eligible for speech and language therapy.

Physical Therapy

Perhaps your baby suffered trauma at birth. Maybe during a routine visit, your pediatrician discovered that your baby has low muscle tone or restricted movement of limbs. Possibly you were concerned as your baby passed the developmental milestone for sitting up or crawling. Then you followed up with a doctor's evaluation and physical therapy was recommended.

Physical therapy deals with "big muscle movements" like sitting, crawling, standing, and walking. Physical therapists are educated in how to exercise and strengthen the large muscles of the body. If your baby receives physical therapy services, you will also be shown exercises to help your child better develop large muscle skills.

 Fact

Physical therapy services typically are scheduled from once to several times a week. Following through with the "homework" is important for your baby, so make this a regular part of your family schedule. Take the PT's lead on how to make the exercises fun. Add your own love, and you will see your baby excel.

Some physical therapists work for doctors, hospitals, schools, and community organizations. It may be necessary to take your baby to office-based physical therapists. Others work for services that come to your home. To find a physical therapist for your baby, talk with your baby's doctor or specialist, or contact a children's hospital in the area where you live. A doctor must prescribe the physical therapist's services.

Occupational Therapy

Some babies are known from birth to need occupational therapy. Perhaps the physical malformation of a hand requires therapy to perform day-to-day tasks like playing with a toy (and later feeding herself, dressing, and writing). Other babies are not identified with a need for occupational therapy until they become toddlers, and have difficulty with play activities or self-care tasks.

 **Question**

How much do therapy sessions cost?
There is no definite answer. If the therapy is part of your baby's Individual Family Service Plan, there will not be a fee. For other kinds of therapy, your family's health insurance and income will be a factor as well as the agency (or individual professional) providing the service.

As with physical therapists, an occupational therapist must have a doctor's prescription before working with a child. Occupational therapists work in offices and, in some cases, provide services in the home.

Speech and Language Therapy

Speech and language milestones for babies and toddlers are perhaps the most misunderstood. Many parents react too quickly and are anxious to begin speech therapy when it is not needed. Other parents are sure that words will come sooner or later. They fail to seek valuable help during the time their child is developing speech and language skills. It's important to remember that developmental milestones are general guidelines and many babies do not mature according to schedule.

If your baby goes beyond the age when most children say their first word, it does not necessarily mean that she needs speech therapy. It is a good idea to touch base with your pediatrician, who may refer your baby for a hearing test or conduct other developmental testing. The important thing is to be aware of your baby's development and to share questions and concerns with appropriate professionals.

Educational Services

In a sense, all therapies are educational for your baby, but some fall into a more traditional education category. These are the therapies that focus on skills you might associate with school learning—color identification or counting, for example.

Developmental Therapy

This education of infants and toddlers is often called *developmental therapy*. The person who provides this service may be a special education teacher or other closely related professional trained in working with children with special needs in the birth-to-age-three population.

Each therapist who works with your baby will make suggestions for practice activities you can do at home. A developmental therapist will incorporate those suggestions into the activities she has planned for your baby. For example, if the occupational therapist is working with your baby to pick things up with a weaker hand, the developmental therapist might use a shape-sorting toy. Your baby would learn how to match shapes at the same time he practices using his weaker hand.

Services for Babies Who Are Deaf or Blind

If your child is deaf or blind, there are additional options for help. Because of the unique, overall needs of these children, education and therapy must be presented in a specific way. For example, a child who is blind is not able to look at a picture book used by a child with normal vision. Rather, the educator might use a variety of tactile items to go along with the story.

Contact your state's early intervention program or state/private schools in your area to find out about programs available for your baby. Often an educator specially trained in teaching the deaf or blind can come to your home. Some schools offer classes on site for babies and their families.

Location

Because therapy and education services for infants and toddlers are offered in a variety of settings, there are pros and cons to consider. Find arrangements that are right for you and your family.

Therapy Services and Medical Offices

Taking your baby to an office for therapy can be convenient if you can combine it with other family activities or if it's near your job. If you take your baby to an office location for therapy, you will meet other families with similar needs. It can be reassuring that you are not the only family facing difficult decisions and schedules. Many lasting friendships (between parents and between children) come about from conversations started in waiting rooms.

 Essential

Sometimes therapy is performed at day care, and at times, may be a necessity. This is not ideal because you cannot see the therapist's example. If you use this kind of arrangement, plan how you will communicate with the therapist. Notes? E-mails? Phone calls? Set up some of the therapy sessions when you will be at home with your baby.

In-Home Services

Early intervention services are often brought to the home. In-home services offer familiarity, comfort, and a different kind of convenience. You do not have to bundle up your baby to take her to an office two or three times a week. You do not have to spend your gas money or get a babysitter for your other children.

Since it is *home*, your baby will feel more at ease. Therapists can often include your baby's own toys in the activities, which you can repeat later.

However, there are some drawbacks to in-home services. Someone, who is initially a stranger, will be coming to your home. Although most families and therapists develop a strong, positive bond, at first the situation can be awkward. There are distractions at home also. The phone continues to ring, neighbors come by, and your other children are competing for your attention. Set up guidelines for family and friends for those times a therapist will be working with your baby.

School Programs

Some schools, particularly those that work with children who are deaf or blind, offer family-oriented classes in which parents participate with their children. These programs focus on teaching families how to communicate with their baby, and how to modify day-to-day activities at home to accommodate their child's special needs.

In some schools there is actually a model "home" in which families practice the communication techniques taught in the program. The guidance and feedback from this realistic setting helps all family members when they return home.

Input

Early intervention services (especially those that are in-home or those that involve the entire family) offer the opportunity for lots of input.

You and your spouse will work with professionals to set up a plan that addresses your greatest concerns. It may be a high priority to your family for your toddler to learn to put on her own socks. You may be most concerned that she understands what "stop" means as you are approaching a street. Another family might be more concerned about their baby's ability to talk.

If the early intervention services are offered in your home, it is important that both parents are present initially when someone comes to work with your baby. That will give both of you the natural opportunity to talk about your goals and concerns for your baby as well as to share your observations.

This is true for other family members as well. Grandparents and siblings can often offer input that is helpful for your baby's therapy. Every therapist knows that a sibling can tell him which toy is the baby's favorite (and which she will likely "work" with).

Participation

A baby very quickly learns who takes care of him. He knows if tears will bring someone running, or if it depends on the situation. In other words, if he cries every night when he is put to bed, will someone immediately run in or will he be given a little time to calm down and give the idea of sleeping a try?

The way you address your baby's special needs is similar. Certainly there are many situations that require immediate attention. Beyond those needs, every baby knows if his parents too quickly coddle and protect.

Parents

Regardless of where your baby gets therapy services, both parents should strive to be involved. Realistically, both parents cannot attend every therapy session. At least one parent must work to bring home the groceries.

So, plan a time to share the strategies with your spouse as soon after each therapy session as possible. Explaining the activities will involve your spouse, and it will also make the directions clearer in your own thinking.

Make arrangements for the other parent to attend at least a few of the sessions. A fresh perspective is always useful. It also tells your baby (no matter how young) that both parents are involved.

Siblings

Infants and toddlers adore their older siblings. Siblings can get a baby to reach for a toy or start to army crawl across the room simply because big brother is doing it.

Siblings do not have to be clever to get a baby's attention. Watch your baby when one of his siblings comes into the room. The sibling will have your baby's undivided attention.

Think about the age of your baby's siblings. What ways can they be involved in working with your baby on his goals? Remember that a baby's work is incorporated in his play activities.

Keep in mind, though, that siblings are also children, and siblings need their own encouragement, time, and attention. Talk to your children about the importance of helping, but also talk to them about things that are important to them as well. The message of who gets Mom and Dad's attention is established very early.

Extended Family and Friends

If your extended family lives nearby, recruit them to help. Grandparents, aunts, and uncles often want to be involved, but often they are not sure what to do. You are your baby's best advocate. Teach those around you about his wants and needs. *You both* need everyone in your baby's life to be involved.

 Essential

The importance of a community working together to meet the needs of children is an established concept. This premise applies especially to children with special needs and *their* community. In order to meet their physical, social, and developmental needs it will take everyone—family, friends, neighbors, and professionals to create an informed and empathetic community.

Like the extended family, friends and neighbors can offer great support. The more they understand about your baby's special needs, the more likely they will be supportive and genuinely helpful. People held at a distance too often misunderstand and can even be judgmental. Friends who are allowed to be involved can add to the number of encouragers for you and your baby.

Exceptions

Regardless of your efforts to involve those around you, some people still will not understand. Some may feel that they "have all the answers" and subsequently try to impose their ideas of what is best for your baby onto you. Others may not see the benefit of all the time and effort you put into helping your baby grow up to his fullest potential. They may believe that a child with a special need does not possess potential. Sadly, this misunderstanding can occur. Focus on those who offer positive support.

Benefits

The clock seems to be running from the moment a baby is born. In fact, it started before the baby's birth. Babies grow quickly and learn quickly. The benefits of early services for your baby are immense.

Early Intervention

The sooner we start the sooner we will get there. If a baby has a hearing loss, she needs amplification as soon as possible. Perhaps she will be able to hear her mother's playful words as she feeds and dresses her. Then she will perhaps be able to start to say some of those words like other babies do.

Being exactly like other babies, even given early intervention, may not always be possible. If the baby's hearing loss is too great, for example, even with amplification she may not hear the playful words that her mother says. She may be able to hear some environmental sounds (like a motorcycle), which may someday save her life, but perhaps not the words of those around her. Nonetheless, early intervention is critical for the baby to learn to make use of her best ability.

Understanding

Your own understanding will also benefit from early services for your baby. Imagine the frustration that so many parents feel, not understanding the cause or nature of their baby's special needs. If they do grasp what is causing the difficulty, they may be wrestling with the ongoing questions: Now what? How do we help our baby?

As you talk with therapists who work with your baby, you will better understand just what your baby is dealing with. Best of all, you will have the opportunity to learn new ideas to try at home.

Awareness

The sooner that intervention begins, the better the opportunity you will have to teach other people in your baby's life. If you understand your baby's needs and how to communicate with, care for, and motivate her, you will be able to share those ideas with other important people in her life.

Your own awareness will also put you in contact with other parents and organizations that can offer support and ideas. By getting involved early, you will have an opportunity to raise awareness in your community. Babies need parents who are advocates and leaders for awareness and change.

Sacrifice

As with any commitment, early intervention for your baby will involve some sacrifice. Early intervention therapy takes time, time that extends beyond the actual appointment. A true commitment to intervention takes time from you, your baby, other family members, and friends.

Schedules

Everyone has a schedule . . . including your baby. As a parent, you prioritize what goes into the schedule and what does not. Work, school, sports, community and religious activities, medical appointments, shopping, and self-care needs crowd the pages of planners. Look at your family's schedule, and put your baby's therapy time high on the list of priorities.

Consistent Effort

Your baby will benefit from ongoing therapy efforts. Perhaps the physical therapist and occupational therapist are working with him to reach for a toy. The activity builds muscle strength, visual focus, and the understanding that with effort he can reach the goal—his toy. Give your baby lots of opportunity to practice. Plan play time.

Look for impromptu occasions to practice the skill as well. For example, did Aunt Sally just give him a great rattle that is colorful and plays a variety of noises? First, let him examine and enjoy the rattle. Then, hold it just out of his reach. Let him use his skills to reach his goal. Following through with therapy takes consistent effort.

At Home

Mom and Dad may be away at work, but the needs of family life at home are constant. Laundry does not go away; it multiplies. Hungry families do not feed themselves. Outside activities call all members of the family. Then there is that pesky little matter of house work. Make a master plan. Divide up the work. Work together. With a plan (and a goal) the things that are really important will get done.

Supplemental Security Income

In addition to therapy, financial help is available to some families. Some babies qualify for government money called *Supplemental Security Income* (SSI). The Social Security Administration outlines several factors determining whether or not a child is qualified:

- **Income and Resources:** Money and other resources available to the child are considered. The government considers if the child can and does work, as well as the financial status of the parents, including their income and the value of their property and other assets.

- **Severity of the Disability:** Children who have had or are predicted to have a disabling condition for at least twelve months qualify for SSI. Children who are not expected to live are also in this category.

Check on Benefits for Your Child

Only the Social Security Administration can determine if your child qualifies. Once you have contacted their office, they will explain the needed information regarding your child's resources and condition. The information will be processed by Disability Determination Services. Check the Social Security Administration website (*www.ssa.gov/pubs/10153.html*) for contact information and application procedures.

 Fact

Following are some of the conditions listed by the Social Security Administration that may qualify a child for SSI: HIV infection, total blindness, total deafness, cerebral palsy, Down syndrome, muscular dystrophy, severe mental retardation (for a child age seven or older), or birth weight below two pounds, ten ounces.

SSI Services Reviewed

Once your child is awarded SSI benefits, the Social Security Administration will periodically review your child's eligibility to receive ongoing assistance. Usually this is done every three years. The review for babies with birth weight under two pounds, ten ounces will occur by the baby's first birthday, except in more severe disabling situations when the review is postponed.

When your child reaches age eighteen, her eligibility is reviewed differently. Some young adults who did not previously qualify based on their parents' income, may do so when they become eighteen but are unable to support themselves.

CHAPTER 7

Discipline Dos and Don'ts

Disciplining a child with special needs is difficult. You must determine fair expectations based on your child's age, disability, and understanding. Sometimes it will be tempting to let discipline slide, especially when you see how hard your child struggles with social interactions and schoolwork. Remember that your goal is to teach your child to be responsible in spite of her disability.

Have a Plan

In order to discipline fairly and appropriately, you have to establish rules. The rules will be very different for a two-year-old with a physical disability and a ten-year-old with ADHD.

Appropriate Considerations

Consider the age of your child. Is he a preschooler who will be learning not to take toys from other children and to talk quietly at the table? Is he an elementary-aged child who will be learning to tell the truth and to be responsible about keeping his room picked up?

Consider the development level of your child when establishing appropriate rules. Even if he is nine years old, he will need some very basic, concrete rules if his cognitive skills are those of a toddler.

Make a List

Decide what behaviors you will address. Here are some areas to consider:

- Physical aggression toward others
- Table manners
- Using kind words
- Completing household chores
- Following directions

Your child will not be able to focus on long lists of rules in every area. Prioritize the rules and begin with the most important. When your child is doing well with those, add more rules to the list.

 Alert

By avoiding discipline, you compound your child's special need. You are encouraging a child who *cannot do* some things to believe that he *does not have to do* other things. He will feel that the rules do not apply to him. But, hearing loss has nothing to do with returning math homework, and ADHD has nothing to do with making his bed.

As you prepare your list of rules, be sure to find out what your spouse's priorities are for your child's behavior. It is important that once you set up the discipline plan, the two of you stick together.

Re-evaluate

Revisit the rules, rewards, and consequences periodically. Use this checklist to help you monitor how the plan is working:

- ✓ Has this behavior plan had a positive effect on your child's behavior?
- ✓ In general, are the rules working?
- ✓ Is your child ready for some new rules?

As your child matures, it will be necessary to change the rules of your discipline plan so they remain appropriate for his age and new behaviors.

Communication

Your child's ability to understand rules is more difficult if her developmental level is very young and her verbal skills are weak. A child cannot obey a rule that she does not comprehend, so you may need to try a variety of ways to make your expectations clear.

Model

Sometimes you will have to show your expectations by almost acting them out. This can be done with family or using dolls or stuffed animals. Two stuffed animals could be used to show that hitting is not okay. One animal hits the other one, making it cry. You say, "Oh no! Kitty hit Spot. Spot is hurt. Spot is sad. Spot is crying."

Look at Kitty and say "No hitting! Spot is hurt! Kitty, you will sit in time-out!" Put Kitty on the same time-out chair that you use for your child. After the time-out is completed remind Kitty to be nice to Spot—no hitting!

Talk

Children with more established verbal skills will respond to an explanation of the expected behavior. Be sure to explain your expectations *beforehand*. For example, you may expect that your child remembers to talk quietly while your family is eating in a restaurant. Explain the expectations before you go to the restaurant. Everyone does better at meeting expectations if they know what the expectations are.

Make a Chart

Many elementary-aged children respond well to a behavior chart. Along one side put simple words or pictures to represent desired behaviors. Across the top write *Morning—Afternoon—Evening*. Give your child a small sticker, draw a happy face, or put a check when the rules are followed. Let her know ahead of time how many marks are necessary to earn a reward.

Written Contracts

Some children do well with a written contract. These are often used in schools for children who have impulsive acting-out behaviors and those with behavior disorders. They can be used with any child who understands the concept.

 Fact

> Many kids need the visual reminder of a chart or a behavior contract. Perhaps your child is impulsive and needs the extra reminder of seeing a chart on your refrigerator. Perhaps your child is on the autism spectrum and verbal reminders are harder to grasp. Visual reminders also help family members remember your child's goals.

A behavior contract will spell out what the child will do or not do. It will state what the rewards or consequences will be. The contract should be easy enough for the child to read. In fact, it is meaningful if the child writes it himself. Then the contract should be signed by both parents and the child.

Follow-Through

Follow-through is an important part of your discipline plan. Without the possibility of a negative consequence, or the hope of a reward, a discipline plan is just words and pictures on a paper. Talk with your spouse about follow-through so that your plan is fully in place as you begin.

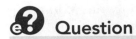

Question

Should a child with ADHD have consequences for his impulsive actions?
His impulsive behavior is in part due to his disability, and yet there should be a certain level of responsibility for his actions. Work with your child on strategies to control his impulsive behavior, but when he is physically aggressive, there should be consequences.

Warnings

Warnings about inappropriate behavior serve a purpose, but if warnings never become consequences, the warnings are meaningless. Two warnings are considered a good number. The first time, you are reminding your child that his behavior is not following a rule that has been explained ahead of time. If the behavior continues, give him a second warning. The second warning tells him that you see the continuing behavior. You mean business. The next step is the consequence. Again, the consequence has been explained well before the situation.

Make Your Words True

Be a parent of true words. Explain your expectations (model, talk, chart, or behavior contract) as well as possible rewards and consequences. Follow through consistently with your spouse. Give two warnings when needed. If the behavior does not change, then the consequence will follow.

Consequences

Make sure that the consequence fits the behavior. For example, your child may be breaking a rule by not clearing his plate off the table. But being grounded would be too severe a consequence for that behavior.

Choosing consequences that are appropriate for your family's discipline plan will depend on your child. Here are some to consider:

- Time-out (This is often done in accordance with the age of the child. A five-year-old might get a five-minute time-out.)
- Missing a preferred activity (DVD, TV program, outside play)
- Early bed time
- Loss of a privilege (cell phone, car, computer)
- Grounding

Try not to have a household or yard job as a consequence. While the hard work will make an impression, you will be telling the child that routine work is a punishment. That is not the mindset you want for future years.

Also try to avoid restricting parent-child bonding time as a consequence. Reading a bedtime story may be a nightly ritual. You and your child have a chance to talk as you build important literacy skills. Taking away that ritual to make a point about his behavior does more damage than good.

Rewards

Rewards should be an easy add-on to the family discipline plan. Truly as much care should be given to the rewards that will be used as to the rules and consequences. Ideally, your child will come to understand that the satisfaction of meeting the expectation is the reward. In the meantime, you will need positive reinforcements that reward desired behavior.

Verbal Praise

Verbal praise is the first and last reward in the sequence of building a healthy desire in your child to follow the rules. Verbal praise should also be used every step of the way. When your child attempts the desired behavior, tell her that she did a good job. Make sure that your words, body language, and facial expressions are all saying the same thing. Use verbal praise often, but only offer it in response to sincere efforts. When you verbally praise your child's half-hearted attempts to do what you ask of her, the compliment will not be as meaningful.

Food Rewards

There are several views on using food as a reward. The habit of rewarding yourself with food when you complete a task is not very healthy. However, for some children with special needs, a food reward is one of the few things that is motivating. This may be true for the child who has a more severe cognitive delay and limited verbal skills. Sometimes small chocolate candies or small crackers (one at a time) are effective. For example, perhaps the child has completed her daily behavior chart and has earned five happy faces at the end of the day. She might be rewarded with five pieces of candy.

 Alert

As soon as your child is interested in other rewards, such as tokens or preferred activities, begin to work those into your discipline plan. You will be fostering healthier eating habits. If your child is resistant to this change, try giving the food reward along with the preferred activity. Gradually phase out the food.

Tokens

Some children like to get a sticker. Perhaps a poster board in your child's room could be used as the sticker poster. Small items can also be used for rewards, including:

- A small toy (given at the end of a week, providing that the required number of positive marks are earned)
- A coin for her bank
- A colorful pencil
- Any small token that is motivating for the child

Preferred Activities

A preferred activity can be used as a reward. It can be something that the child does during a typical day but would love to do more (such as watching a DVD). It can also be a preferred activity that is used only for reward (blowing bubbles in the backyard). Again, the motivation and appropriateness of the activity depends on the child.

Special Outings and Events

Consider a special outing or event as a larger reward. Perhaps your child likes to eat at a popular hamburger place. That might be a reward at the end of a good week. Perhaps your child wants to visit the zoo. Again, that would be a reward after a block of time.

Younger children need rewards after shorter periods of time. "You did a great job this morning. Let's play on the swings before lunch." Older children can work for a reward over time.

Consistency

Consistency is important in order to effectively influence your child's behavior. If the rule sometimes stands and sometimes does not, it will be tempting to take the risk. The child who really wants to play on the computer when he is supposed to be doing homework, for example, will be more tempted to do so if there are consequences only some of the time.

Between Parents

One of the first ways that your child will test the consistency of your rules is to compare how each parent enforces them. It may happen when your child is a toddler and wants to take his juice into the living room, for example. Perhaps the rule is that the juice stays in the kitchen. Mom enforces the "no juice in the living room" rule. Your toddler wants to know if the rule holds on Saturday afternoon when Mom is out and Dad is in charge. He may not have the verbal skills to say that, but his behaviors will test it out.

Whether or not juice is in the living room may be the least of your concerns. The fact is that your child will retest the consistency between parents from time to time. In fact, he will become a more frequent tester the more times he can get away with it.

Another thing to consider about the consistency between parents is the age of your child. As he gets older and goes through normal stages of emotional independence, he will be much more likely to test between parents if there is a history of success.

Be consistent. It is important that both parents reinforce the rules and each other. When your child has the needed verbal skills, remind him that a no from one parent means no from the other.

Different Times, Different Places

Are your rules the same at different times and in different places? Do you have consistent rules at home but not so much in public? Perhaps you are pretty consistent on the weekends, but during the week the work rush sweeps some of the rules out of the door.

You may not be able to immediately follow through on "time-out" discipline when you are in the checkout line at the grocery store. Your child will learn to respect your reminder that the consequence will happen as soon as you are at home, if you are consistent with follow-through regardless of where the incident takes place.

Day Care and School

Sometimes there is a difference in the way discipline is applied at home and in other places—like day care and school. You can address some of the difference. If you are hiring a babysitter to care for your child, you can explain your family's discipline system.

When your child is in a group situation, you will not have as much control over the rules and consequences. Think about homework rules in your child's classroom. Perhaps the rule is to make up missing homework at lunch recess. You know that your child is struggling with math concepts, but he could complete the work with a little explanation at home. Tonight your child has soccer practice, and that will cut into the homework time. You have some choices:

- Have him miss practice in order to complete the work.
- Let him go to practice and then "help" him complete the work by talking him through each answer.
- Let him go to the practice, and then complete his work for him.
- Understand that there will be a consequence at school for the unfinished work.

If you choose to do his work or coax him through the answers, he learns that he is not accountable for the expectations at school. His rules are not consistent.

There is a time, as a parent, to speak up if the rules at day care or school are not fair. That is another topic. The concern here is on communicating rules and applying them consistently across the areas of your child's life.

Between Siblings

It is normal for siblings to feel that the other one has fewer rules or that the rules are not enforced equally. This can be even more of an issue if one child has a special need. The other siblings may feel that the child with a special need gets away with things.

Have rules that are developmentally appropriate for each sibling. A child with Down syndrome may be expected to put his dirty laundry in a clothes basket. His sister may be expected to sort the laundry for the whole family and to wash the towels. The difference in rules should be developmentally appropriate.

It may be necessary to explain to your family that rules are based on ability and age. Assure your other children that you will fairly enforce the rules for all. Consistent expectations and consequences will make this rule setup as fair as possible.

Let's Start Again

There is an old saying about not throwing the baby out with the bath water. Children make mistakes. (Don't we all!) They will test the rules and the people who are enforcing the rules.

Discipline is a way to reinforce your expectations, but needing to discipline your child does not mean that she is bad. Know when and how to give your child a fresh start. She will be watching to see when she has been forgiven, and your unconditional love is critical to her emotional growth.

 Fact

Children with special needs thrive on structure. Having a well-thought-out discipline plan and following it is a great way to provide structure for your child. Her world becomes more predictable, and predictable is understandable. She will begin to understand the consequences of not obeying, and learn greater responsibility for her actions.

Put an End to the Discipline

As you establish a fair, consistent discipline plan you will see a beginning and an end to each behavior incident. For example, suppose your child willfully ignores your request to pick up her toys. You ask a second time, but still no effort is made to pick up the toys. Finally, you remind her of the consequence: no TV for the evening. You are consistent and follow through on your word; there is no TV that evening.

The next thing in your family's nightly routine is bath, story, and bed. Remember that the behavior is finished. The discipline is finished. Approach the remainder of the evening with a fresh start. Treat her refusal to pick up her toys as if it had never happened.

Have a Fresh Start—Review the Expectations

Here is how the fresh-start scenario works:

- Your child breaks the rules.
- You give your child a warning about her behavior. You remind her that she is not following your expectations.
- The behavior continues.
- You remind her again.
- The behavior continues.
- You tell her that there will be no TV that evening.
- At the end of the usual TV time, you explain that you are disappointed (or sad) that she did not follow the rules. That is why she did not have TV. Explain that you know that next time she will pick up her toys when you ask.
- Continue with the night-time routine without further reminder of the incident. It is time for a fresh start.

Disciplining a Tween

Things get a little more complicated as kids enter the tween and teen years. (Okay—they get a lot more complicated!) Your little child who (possibly reluctantly) complied with your requests will seem to have vanished. Rest assured that special need or not, the tween/teen years will be emotional and challenging.

The Age of the Tween

Tweens are going through hormonal changes. They are expressing a new level of independence from their parents. Often they seem to challenge or rebel against everything, from what to wear, to what they say, and who they want to hang out with. Your child will experience many changes in the emotional tween years.

Tween Discipline Plan

Continue to explain your expectations as your child enters this period. Remember that your discipline plan has been changing as your child has grown and matured. Make sure that your tween is very clear on your expectations.

 Alert

Your tween will go through the same hormonal changes as his peers, although he may not have the language skills to understand the changes. Make sure to include your expectations concerning interaction with the opposite sex in your discipline plan. Too often, this area is overlooked, and avoidable, socially inappropriate situations arise.

Here are some things that you will want to have in your tween's discipline plan (note that some of them are on the list for younger children as well):

- Language
- Household chores
- Curfew
- Acceptable places to go
- Cell phone use
- Internet use
- Boy-girl issues
- Smoking and drugs

Keep your discipline consistent. Just like your plan when your child was young, your discipline plan should include reminders, rewards, and consequences.

CHAPTER 8

Part of a Family

Some children with special needs are born into large, supportive, extended families. Some function in a single-parent home with little support. Others are adopted into a family that is ready to take on the challenges of raising a child with special needs. Certain basic ground rules and goals can help your family address the needs of your child and each of his family members. Having a plan can head off family upset and stalemates.

Time and Attention

Attention from other people is a basic human need, important to our emotional well-being. This is why children who live in orphanages with minimal human contact may show delayed physical, emotional, cognitive, and verbal development. Most children with special needs, of course, do not come from a neglectful environment. Their parents are quick to agree that having a child with a special need means extra time and attention, from breakfast time in the morning to homework time in the evening. How do parents manage to meet the needs of their child as well as the rest of the family? Time and attention for each of your children must be a priority. Find out what works for your family.

Your Child Needs Time and Attention

Talk with your spouse about the time, attention, and care that your child needs. Consider all of the basic areas of need:

- Eating
- Rest times and bedtime schedule
- Bathing, dressing, and personal care
- Appointments
- Schoolwork
- Practice for various therapies
- Family fun time
- Exercise
- Activities in the community
- Time to chill

Plan how you will divide up the parenting responsibilities. It is important that you both take part in your child's care. If both parents do not take an active role, your child will feel left out by the other parent.

Plan Time for Siblings

Likewise, her siblings will feel resentful of parents who spend all of their time caring for the child with special needs. Most children understand that their sibling has extraordinary needs, but they do not understand when those needs take up all of Mom or Dad's time. Siblings have needs, too. They need parental support and guidance in difficult times. They need a parent's praise when they have done well.

Children do not raise themselves. Talk with your spouse about the basic needs of your other children. Have a game plan for which parent will do what. The plan does not have to be rigid, but it is a starting point when things get hectic.

Make Time for Your Spouse

Between the common demands of work, activities, running a home, and taking care of children, things can get very hectic. For example, if a child in the family has a special need such as ADHD, a little homework can take a lot of time.

It is imperative that you make time for you and your spouse. Plan some time together, and put it into your family schedule. Things that are on a schedule get done, but good intentions may not. Occasionally plan time with your spouse away from your family. Even a short getaway for frozen yogurt will help your relationship and how you deal with family responsibilities.

Include Extended Family

Plan time with your extended family. Welcome them into activities and care for your child and her siblings. Consider accepting help from extended family members and friends to meet the needs of each of your children. Additionally, remember that they have needs as well. Do something for them to repay their generosity.

Schedules that Work

You may have given a lot of thought to your child's schedule. You know when he needs to be in bed so he won't be overly tired the next day. You know when he goes to physical therapy. You know which day of the week his spelling sentences are due.

Make a point to think about the overall family schedule. Obviously no one lives in isolation of his family members. The full family schedule also needs to work.

Everyday Schedules

Planning the day-to-day routines helps the family function. Think about mealtimes that work for the group. If your child needs assistance with eating, you may need to plan a two-part meal schedule—one for the whole family and one for the parent who helped with feeding so that he can finish his meal.

Things really do work more smoothly if they happen at the same time and in the same order every day. Put bath and bed times in your overall schedule. If everyone anticipates what is happening next you have won half of the battle. You don't have to convince or remind the children that it's bath time, for example.

Extracurricular Schedules

Some families have extracurricular activities every day of the week. Some of them have back-to-back activities any given evening. If you have a child who needs extra time to complete the basic activities (homework, supper, family time, bath, and bed), extracurriculars can be tricky.

 **Alert**

Often children with learning disabilities feel overwhelmed with homework and extracurricular activities. Try choosing one activity that is really important to your child. If possible, have him participate in a weekend activity. If he knows that he has scouts on Thursday nights, he can finish his long-range homework on other evenings.

Think about the individual needs of each of your kids. Think about their ages, their homework loads, and their stamina in the evenings. Wouldn't it be better to have fewer activities and have everyone enjoy them instead of planning and committing every waking moment?

Sometimes parents split up the activities, with one parent going to one activity and the other parent going to a different one. Sometimes one parent goes to the activities, and the other one stays home with the other children. That plan works sometimes, but if you never see each other and no one has a clue what is for supper, your family is overextended.

Communicating the Schedule

Make sure that everyone understands the schedule. Children on the autism spectrum, particularly, are not fond of change. Sometimes change is so upsetting to them that everyone feels their pain as they act out impulsively. They thrive on routine. The world is tricky to figure out, and new situations mean that they are continually trying to do that. Get a family calendar. Talk to your child and communicate the schedule.

Chores and Responsibilities

"Because you are a part of this family!" Parents have used this familiar response for generations. People who are part of a family are expected to pitch in and help. You are not running a motel. Everybody has his part to play.

Choosing Chores

The chores that you give your child should match her age as well as her developmental and physical skills. A child in a wheelchair might be able to use a feather duster. A child who is on the autism spectrum might sort items to be recycled.

It is helpful to choose a small group of chores and then add to them over time. Once she has mastered a set of chores, perhaps your child can rotate them with a sibling. This week one of the children may unload the dishwasher and vacuum the living room. Next week, she will load the dishwasher and collect the dirty laundry. Her sibling will do the other chores.

Communicating Your Expectations

Use the communication techniques you have learned for discipline and general rules: model, talk, or use a visual like a chart.

Charts work especially well for chores because each one can be marked off as it is completed. You and your child can tell at a glance how things are going.

Rewarding Chores

Parents have differing opinions on whether children should be paid for doing chores. No matter which side of the fence you are on, rewarding a job well done is important for the child with special needs. Ultimately, you will want your child to take care of her responsibilities because it is the right thing to do.

Chores can be rewarded with money, depending on the work that is actually done. Perhaps your child's chores include taking out the garbage and feeding the dog, but she only took out the garbage. Her payment should be lower because she did not complete all of her tasks.

Some families reward chores with a family activity. If Saturday is work-around-the-house day, perhaps the family reward is going to the park when the work is completed, or maybe inviting guests over for the evening.

Pets

Pets offer unconditional love. Pets can also teach responsibility. Since a pet is a big commitment, and you can't easily give it back, consider whether a pet is right for your child and your whole family.

Expense

Is your family ready for the expense of a pet? That may seem like an odd consideration in a book on parenting a child with special needs. But think about the things you will need to pay for: food, bed, cage, toys, and veterinarian visits. They can add up. If you have been wishing that you had a little extra cash to buy more easy-reader books for your child who is struggling to read, you may opt not to buy that pet. If you can't pass up the benefit and enjoyment your child will receive from having a pet, borrow those books from the library, and go ahead and get the pet.

 Essential

Think too about who will exercise and play with the pet. Will it get enough play time with people? Helping your child play with an animal can offer lots of great conversation starters and opportunities to practice words and sentences without even thinking about it.

Feeding

Someone has to take the time to feed a pet. Feeding the cat or the dog can be a great way to teach your child empathy and responsibility. It can give him a feeling of importance in the family. However, if you are struggling to get people to clear their own plates off the table, adding another mouth to the household may not be a good idea.

My Pet—My Buddy

Many pets are helpful for their owners. Of course, there are specially trained dogs to assist older teens and adults. Some pets are just naturally helpful, even without special training. Rewarding the dog for letting a child who is deaf know that someone is calling is well worth the minimal effort involved.

Sibling Rivalry

Sibling rivalry is largely based on the perception of time and attention. No matter their ages, siblings seem always to have one eye on whether things seem fair. Often, there can be resentment toward a child with special needs; it may feel like Mom is paying more attention to the sibling who needs a little more help.

It is important to spread the time and attention around. It is also important for your child to devote some time and attention for his siblings. While you don't want to overload activities, it is a good idea to have your child attend at least some of his siblings' activities (games, programs, etc.).

Make sure that all of your children are on the family team, so to speak. Everyone should encourage the others. Everyone should be excited when someone accomplishes a goal, and everyone should be sympathetic when things don't go right.

Parent Travel

When a parent must travel (even occasionally), it can leave a giant hole in how things function at home. Activity schedules, homework, and even meals can send the family scrambling to make things work when one parent is absent.

The Upset

A child who is easily upset by change can suffer the most. The home is often the one place where the child feels as if she knows how things operate. The surroundings are familiar and the routines comforting. When a parent is gone, the comfort zone is disturbed.

A child who is nonverbal may suddenly begin to act out. Her actions say: "I don't understand or like what is happening." A child who has Asperger's syndrome may suddenly become preoccupied. Her focus at school can be drastically different than the norm. At home, she may ask repeatedly about the absent parent. It is not that she doesn't understand that the parent is gone; it is just very upsetting to the predictability of her world.

Avoiding the Upset

As much as possible, let your child know in advance about who will be gone. You may have a family calendar that can help your child visualize the time period when the parent will be away. Assure your child that the absence is only temporary. Realize that even with discussion ahead of time, your child's world will still be upset. You will likely see some evidence of her feelings through her behaviors.

Getting Back to Normal

Even if the absence is a few hours in the afternoon, a time of readjustment may be necessary. If you were the missing parent, your child may initially seem happy to greet you; then she may switch to avoiding you. She is letting you know that she was not happy that you were gone. It may seem like she is punishing you. Be pleasant and available so she can let you back into her world. Assure her that you are happy to be home. Plan some special time to do something you enjoy doing together.

Family Illness

People get sick. Sometimes illness can be short-term, and sometimes illness can be very serious—even to the point of death. When the person who is ill is a close family member or when it is someone close to the child's caregiver, the impact on the child can be immense.

A family member who is ill may look very scary to your child. Someone who is normally caring and positive may be unable to address the usual needs of the child. Your child may not have the language skills to understand what is happening, or even if the illness is temporary (Mom's flu) or long-term (Uncle's cancer).

 Alert

Just the physical appearance of the loved one may be upsetting. Seeing medical equipment connected to a loved one can also be upsetting. A child with severe language or cognitive impairments may even try to pull the alarming tubes and wires off of the person. The child may think that she is freeing the person who is sick.

How much information you share with your child will largely depend on his age and abilities. He may enjoy making cards or drawing pictures for the patient. By engaging in an activity, he may feel as if he is helping the situation.

Rely on familiar caregivers to help out until your family is back to normal. Someone who knows your child's routine, communication, behavior, likes and dislikes, and medication considerations will be able to step into the situation. It is always critical to have a caregiver who can do these things. Waiting to find someone at the time of your own illness may be impossible.

Births

The birth of a sibling can be exciting. Keep in mind that it is also a change in your child's life—a change in her routine and a change in the family structure. To make the transition as smooth as possible, have a plan that will begin before your new baby is born and continue for several months after her birth.

 Fact

With enough preparation for a new baby, a sibling with special needs can be resilient or at least accepting over time. Life is full of changes. Part of being successful is learning to accept the changes and to go on. Accepting the new baby may be a big task for your child, but she can do it!

Preparing for the Baby

No doubt, you have read about how to prepare siblings for a new arrival. The process is much the same if one sibling has a special need. The part that is different is *how* the information is communicated.

Remember that your child may need visual communication. As she notices that Mommy's tummy is getting larger, introduce baby pictures. Show her pictures of herself: Mommy's tummy, pictures or videos of her in the womb, newborn pictures, and recent ones. Show her the celebration of her birth.

Next, remind her of Mommy's growing tummy. Share photos or videos of the new sibling in the womb. Then visit the room that will be the baby's nursery. Encourage her to share in the joy of the coming birth. If your child has an events calendar, add a picture of a baby to the top of the month when she will be born.

Time as a Family

Allow for extra family time before the new baby's birth and afterward as well. Your child wants to see that she fits into this picture and may not be able to tell you her concerns. Involve your child in the care of the baby, but also show her that *you* will continue to care for her as well. Make a point to give the baby to your spouse and get your child a drink or help her with bedtime. Remember that for the child who is visually oriented, actions do speak louder than words.

One-on-One Parent Time

Plan one-on-one time with your child after the baby's birth. This can be done at home, or with short outings. It is especially important to include things that you have enjoyed doing together in the past. Your child is always trying to figure out what is the same and what has changed in her life. Knowing that her favorite activities with Mommy or Daddy will continue is an important part of her accepting her new sibling.

Sibling Jealousy Throughout the Years

Sibling jealousy has some part in every family. As your children get older, some of the circumstances around the jealousy will change. When "typically developing" siblings start extracurricular activities or when they can go places with friends, your child may get frustrated. Life can seem so unfair. Talk with her about her activities and privileges. Remind her that Mom and Dad are proud of her accomplishments as well.

Divorce

The emotional and financial strain of having a child with a special need can place stress on a marriage. Separation and divorce is not uncommon. Your child will struggle to understand what is happening and how he fits into the new lives of both parents.

Time Together

Your child needs as many fans on his side as possible. He will struggle with schoolwork and social situations even more than his peers. As he faces obstacles and gains success, let him know that you are both on his side.

 Essential

Lots of information sharing, brainstorming, and planning happens at school IEP meetings. If possible, both parents should attend so that they can give input and provide the follow-through that the child needs. If this is not possible, share your child's IEP documents, professional evaluations, and progress reports with your ex-spouse.

Time with Each Parent

Depending on the visitation agreement, the child will spend some time with each parent. It is important that the noncustodial parent understands the child's needs. Both parents should be comfortable with his communication so that the child's wants and needs are understood. Also, both parents should work to consistently address the child's speech and language goals. Strive for consistent discipline between households. This is important for any child, but consistent expectations are especially important for the child who struggles to understand change.

Stepparents

Often a stepparent will have some responsibility for the child. Adequate information about communication, discipline, and goals should be shared by all parents. The more consistent your child's world, the better he will be able to cope and develop to his fullest potential. Set up a way to communicate back and forth about these areas.

Having a communication notebook that travels between parents' homes can take some of the emotional charge out of the situation. Many parents are reluctant to use a notebook because they feel that their actions will be criticized or used against them. Try to stick to the facts and communicate primarily about such things as the agreed-upon schedule, illness, and homework.

Death

Death is difficult to explain even to a child without a special need. The emotional toll on all family members will make the loss even harder for your child. Those who typically offer support and try to explain what is happening can be at a loss themselves.

If the loss is expected, you will obviously have more time to prepare your child. It may not be appropriate for your child to visit the relative who is ill.

Talk with your child using family photos. Explain that you are sad. Incorporate your family's religious beliefs on a very basic level.

Sometimes a loss is sudden. The loss will be jarring to you, but it will be even more upsetting to a child who looks for consistency in her world. Again, use the basics of your religious beliefs. Also, be prepared to explain as situations come up that would have involved the loved one: daily activities, child care, visits, holidays, and birthdays.

The Visitation and Funeral

Consider whether or not your child is ready to attend the visitation and the funeral. Some children do not have the emotional or cognitive maturity to handle either situation.

Another child may be able to go to a private visitation where you can be more readily available to her and where she can have more time. The child may not be ready for a group situation of a funeral. Some children are able to attend both the visitation and the funeral.

A Healing Season

Expect that your child will need time to heal from her loss, just as you will. Allow extra time around the periods that she would have had contact with the loved one. If Aunt Sally normally babysat on Saturday afternoons while you bought groceries, expect that Saturdays will be especially difficult—for both of you.

Remember that your child may express her grief in a number of ways. She may be visibly sad or she may be able to express her feelings in words. She may, however, handle her frustration by acting out.

CHAPTER 9

Teaching Family Traditions

Every family has its own way of doing things. From celebrating birthdays to doing the laundry, families are grounded in tradition. A child with special needs works hard to understand the world around her. Since traditions are visual and repeat regularly, most children with special needs "know the routine." Your child likely knows your family's traditions but may not be able to explain them. She may not be able to discuss times that they will be different from the norm. Read on for ways to help your child better understand and learn from your family's traditions.

Example

"Actions speak louder than words" as the old saying goes. People learn better from a role model than a list of dos and don'ts. This is especially true for children who struggle to understand words. Children with developmental delays learn that hitting is wrong. They do not see their parents hitting others. If they themselves hit a sibling, immediate negative responses come from parents (frowns, scolding, discipline) and from the sibling (crying, anger, hitting back). Children with special needs learn from those around them how they should act.

Most children also learn from facial expressions. They recognize a positive response of approval, a questioning look of

103

confusion, a look of caution, and so on. This carries over to their understanding of traditions. If it looks like Mom truly enjoys and values a tradition, it must be important. If it looks like she has a grin-and-bear it attitude, maybe it is not such a good habit.

The specific disability of the child further complicates the importance of facial expressions. For some, facial expressions are vital. For others, facial expressions have little or no meaning. For example:

- Children on the autism spectrum and many children with behavior disorders are less aware of facial expressions. Other times children with behavior disorders *do* understand an expression, but choose not to be influenced by it.
- Children who are deaf and those with severe cognitive delays rely heavily on facial expressions to make up for the words that they do not hear clearly.
- Children with severe cognitive disabilities quickly read the sentiment behind the expression.

Make faces at yourself in the mirror! Does your "you did a great job" face look like it is saying congratulations? Although this sounds odd, sometimes a look that is meant to be approving looks almost sympathetic. By the same token, a disapproving look can look mean. Make sure your mug is communicating your thoughts.

Pictures

Besides facial expressions and role models, pictures are worth a thousand words to a child who watches the world and yet has not mastered its language. Use pictures to explain your words about things that are not in the room with you.

Collect pictures that relate to your child's life. Photographs, calendars, magazines, catalogs, Internet pictures and graphics, greeting cards, stickers, labels from food products, and drawings are a few sources for easy-to-get pictures.

Use Pictures to Talk about Family Traditions

Use photos of past experiences to talk about upcoming activities and occasions. Make use of multiple print options at the photo store, print select pictures with your printer at home, or let your child view them on the computer screen.

Consider using a picture next to your child's calendar to signal something very special, such as a birthday, house guest, or vacation. Be sure to talk to your child about what will be different this time around. For example, last year you went to the beach on vacation. This year you will go camping.

Stickers are useful when marking special events on the calendar or creating reminder notes. You may want to communicate: *Wear your green pants* [green sticker with word] *and yellow shirt* [yellow sticker with word].

Create food cards by gluing product pictures on index cards. Talk with your child about the list for your trip to the store: "We need milk. We need bread. We need soup." Point to each picture card as you talk.

Calendars

Your family's overall activities teach tradition. If your children are on sports teams and you have season tickets for sports events, sports are obviously part of your family's traditions. If your family camps every weekend or rides bikes after dinner each evening, you obviously love the outdoors. You do what you love. You get the picture. Most kids with special needs "get the picture" better if they know what is happening next.

Children on the autism spectrum are easily overwhelmed with new situations. Those with ADHD are thrown off by unexpected events and activities. Having a calendar to show the plan is a great way to build communication and increase family fun.

Create a Basic Calendar

A family-friendly calendar should be fairly large. It will need to have enough room for some wording, times, small pictures, and stickers. Poster board, sheets of large sturdy paper, or a desk/blotter type calendar work well.

If you are making a calendar from scratch, clearly print the name of each month as well as the numbers for the days. Another way to embellish the calendar is to let your child cut out the month names and pictures from an old calendar. Ready-made calendars that have pictures showing something significant about the month work well. For example, July might have a picture of fireworks.

Things to Include on the Calendar

Use your own calendar to get you started for ideas. Basically, anything that is not part of your regular everyday routine is a good fit for the calendar.

The key is to keep it short and to the point. If Grandma will babysit on Tuesday and Thursday evenings while you are at class, put a small picture of Grandma on those days with a time. If physical therapy will be three days this week, print *PT* and the time. If physical therapy is normally Monday, Wednesday, and Friday, but Wednesday's session is cancelled this week, write it on all three of the days and then cross out the Wednesday listing.

Marking the Calendar

Include your child in creating and marking the calendar. This should be done with supervision. You don't want drawings, scribbles, or seventy-five stickers covering the month of November!

Depending on the age and fine motor skills of your child, he may help mark the calendar by:

- Labeling the months, days, and numbers
- Cutting out and gluing names of the months and seasonal pictures from magazines and old calendars

- Using stickers to mark special days (bus stickers for school days, candle stickers for birthdays)
- Crossing off the days before an event, such as a birthday

The everyday tradition of using a family calendar will boost your child's communication skills and will reduce his frustration by helping him to understand what is happening.

Everyday Traditions

Remember the poem about children learning what they live? This rings true for children with special needs as well as others. In fact, the habits of your family will teach your child many of society's expectations.

 Fact

Experts estimate that it's necessary to do something thirty to fifty times before it becomes a habit. Pick one habit that you would like to "teach" your child. Challenge yourself and other family members to be role models for your child. When that habit is established, choose another one for your family goal. Life is so much easier with good habits!

Your child sees every aspect of life in your home. This includes "school skills" such as reading, writing, and arithmetic! Here are some other kinds of habits your child will learn at home:

- Empathy/forgiveness
- Conversation
- Confidence
- Manners/hospitality
- Self-care (brushing teeth, washing face, showers)
- Diet/exercise

- Housecleaning/yard care
- Recycling
- Finances/shopping
- TV/computer time

A good or bad example can be shown in each of the areas. Remember that you are your child's main teacher.

Family Fun

The importance of planning a family fun time may seem obvious. Very often, families today are so busy that family fun becomes a good intention that is overshadowed by outside activities, therapies, school, work, sports—the list goes on.

Having a child with a special need impacts the entire family. Parents are faced with many critical decisions. Children with special needs work hard—very hard—to accomplish the same things that come easily for other children. Their hard work often requires time and attention from Mom and Dad. Siblings can easily feel slighted when it comes to their parents' attention. Planning family fun times can pull the family back together and provide much needed relaxation.

Backyard Fun

You don't have to actually have a backyard to have backyard fun. The idea is to look for simple, everyday fun around your own home. Here are some ideas for backyard fun:

- Blow bubbles
- Draw with sidewalk chalk
- Ride bikes
- Play catch
- Plant a flower
- Read under a tree

Backyard fun usually doesn't cost anything, and it is a great filler for times your child is looking for something to do.

Movie Night

Life is busy. Too many things on the to-do list can be stressful for everyone. This is especially true for children who are overwhelmed with social situations, such as children on the autism spectrum. Family movie night offers laid-back family fun.

Just being together is an important element to building a strong family. Children with developmental delays often respond well to the animation and songs of old-fashioned family movies.

 Essential

Some children on the autism spectrum become obsessed with a particular movie. They want to see it over and over. Often they have lines of the script memorized. As parents, discuss the guidelines for family movie night. If your child watches another movie, will she then be allowed to watch her favorite?

Pick a regular evening without outside activities and without the possibility of lots of homework to have family movie night. A weekend evening often fits the bill as your family celebrates the end of a busy week or chills before the new week begins.

Games Galore

Declare a certain night game night. Many games are great skill builders whether your child is working on counting, answering questions, or managing money! Of course, many are just plain fun.

The object of game night is increasing family time together and strengthening family bonds. Everyone looks forward to a shared activity. Everyone shares a common goal (win that game). Game night builds family bonds, but it also builds personal confidence and teamwork.

Make food a part of the game night fun. Game night can also be pizza night, or you can work with your child to make special snacks the night before.

Make a Treat

Basic cooking skills are important for life. Making a treat does not mean you have to bake something from scratch (although you can). Making a special treat with your child teaches the following skills:

- Reading—following directions
- Sequence—the order that the steps should be done
- Math—fractions, time, temperature
- Creativity—decorating, planning menus

Children with special needs take pride in their work. It is especially important when they can make something for someone they love.

Birthdays

How does your family celebrate birthdays? Children, even those with limited language skills, remember the details of family traditions like birthdays. This is another opportunity to tell your child that he is an important member of the family.

Planning the Celebration

Stick with the party traditions of your family. If you always have a balloon centerpiece, party hats, and noise makers, be sure to have these ready to go. If you always have a dinner with cake and ice cream, plan the same for your child's birthday. If the cousins, aunts and uncles, and grandparents gather for other birthdays, be sure to plan the same type of gathering for your child.

Plan the family gathering at a time when your child is at his best. Keep in mind that the overall activity may need to be shorter based on your child's physical stamina. The important thing is to have the celebration. If your child's cousins came to his brother's birthday, he will remember that they came to his. He will not be watching the clock to make sure that everyone stayed the same amount of time.

School-aged children may enjoy a party with friends. Many children with learning disabilities have friends from their inclusion class as well as from the special education classroom. Party time is a great opportunity to forget about special education needs and encourage your child to mix with other children regardless of disability. Plan a party that will focus on things he loves to do, such as dancing or swimming.

 Alert

Check with the parents of children who will attend the birthday party about allergies to peanuts, chocolate, and other foods. Some children are allergic to the latex found in most balloons and many party favors. Add a note near the RSVP number on the invitation: *Please help us plan a safe party. . . . Does your child have any allergies?*

Some children have friends primarily from their special education program. This might be because of developmental delay or in some cases because of communication. Consider a party for these close friends. This may be a little trickier to set up because these families are often from a larger area than the neighborhood school, but bear in mind that these are your child's friends.

Gifts

Buying gifts for a ten-year-old with developmental delays or a four-year-old who has not yet started to speak can be a challenge. Consider four things when purchasing birthday gifts for your child.

- What are my child's interests?
- What is my child's developmental level?
- What is my child's language ability?
- How old is my child?

If you still need great gift ideas, talk to your child's teacher, speech therapist, occupational therapist, or physical therapist. There are many wonderful games and toys that are fun yet helpful in building skills.

 Essential

Keep in mind that friends and family may also need guidance about appropriate gifts. Having a wish list, sharing a catalog with marked gift ideas, or creating a gift registry at a toy store can help. In some cases, you may want to offer to do the shopping for relatives who want to choose just the right gift.

Every gift does not have to be educational. Every gift does not have to be only for fun. Try to get a mix to address the overall needs and wants of your child.

Holidays

Holidays offer an opportunity to teach traditions that include giving and receiving, family celebrations, and decorations.

Choosing Decorations

Most families have favorite decorations that are used year after year. Again, for many children with special needs this is a situation of visual importance. Your child may not understand the reason behind the traditions, but she will most likely notice if the usual door decoration is missing or hung in a different location.

Many kids on the autism spectrum are overly interested in decorations of a certain color or type. Trains are often in this category. Children with autism also love dangling decorations. Include some of these favorite decorations that your child can enjoy year after year.

Preserve the tradition by keeping most of the decorations the same. Include your child in displaying the decorations. Introduce one or a few new decorations as a ritual for every year. Then the change (adding new decorations) becomes a part of the tradition.

Holiday Gifts

Follow the tips for birthday gifts when shopping for your child for the holidays. Let your child help in shopping and giving to others. When preparing gifts to give, have your child add a gift tag or bow. Let her put the gift in its place until the gift exchange begins.

Traditions Away from Home

Holiday seasons can be packed with activities, parties, programs, and shopping. Consider the following questions before committing to another event:

- Is this a good time of day for my child?
- Are we enjoying a balance of at-home and away-from-home activities?
- Would a different activity be better suited to my family?
- Should I make arrangements for child care while I attend this?

Remember that you and your child do not have to attend every holiday event. Choosing carefully will make the season more enjoyable and meaningful for the entire family.

In general, keep the holidays simple. The more complicated the plans, the less likely it will be a perfect holiday. Focus your expectations on time with those you love.

Teaching with Traditions

Traditions are your family's footprint on your child's life memories. Whether or not he knows the words behind the traditions, he understands that the habits are important. As his language skills increase, you will have a better opportunity to explain the rationales and beliefs behind your family's habits.

Later, your child may question or even reject the traditions of your family. This is not uncommon in the rebellious teen years. But the memories of your family traditions will remain a constant.

Often it is those traditions that give a child a sense of self and purpose as an adult. It is surprising how many children come back to the traditions of their family when they have their own children.

When Traditions Vary

Let's face it, life is not always predictable. When something unavoidable comes up, a family tradition can be very different or may not even happen. Let's suppose that your family always has movie night on Friday. You always eat pizza. Mom, Dad, and kids get comfy with sleep pants and pillows. It is a great family fun time. But this week Dad is called out of town for work. You will need to choose if movie night will happen this time without Dad or if you will move it to another evening.

Communicate Early

Surprises are overrated. This is especially true for children who are struggling to make sense of day-to-day routine. Throw a change of plans into the works and everyone will be frustrated.

As soon as you know that a family tradition will be different, plan when to tell your child. It is not necessary to tell her right away. If you find out three months in advance that Grandpa cannot come for her birthday, for example, it is too early to have the discussion. It is important, however, to be honest and to give your child enough notice that she will get used to (not necessarily like) the idea of the change.

 Fact

> Being upset about change is a common characteristic of children with autism, learning disability, behavior disorder, and developmental delay. If your child is upset because of change, it does not mean she falls into one of these categories. Some children may not easily understand verbal explanations and therefore seek consistency. Others are overwhelmed with new situations.

Let Your Child Help Change the Calendar

Children with special needs often feel as if they have little control over their lives. Truly, their days are filled with appointments, therapies, school, homework, and plain old responsibilities. Having your child help make the needed changes on the calendar gives her a sense of control in a situation that is ultimately out of her control.

If you have decided to have the activity without the person important to your child, keep things upbeat. In the situation where Dad was traveling on family movie night, perhaps Dad can be the one to take your child to the store to rent the movies before he leaves. Perhaps Dad can leave a note on the special snacks explaining how excited he is about the next movie night.

Help your child mark the next movie night on the calendar. Reinforce that Dad will be at that movie night. Keep reinforcing the idea as that night approaches.

CHAPTER 10

Out and About— Social Situations

Your family may include several children as well as extended family members, or you may have only one child. You may live in a busy metropolitan area or in the country. You may work outside of the home or you may be a stay-at-home parent. It really doesn't matter what your family's situation is, sooner or later you will be out with your child and dealing with social situations. Have personal guidelines and goals for yourself, your child, and those around you for these situations.

More Actions and Reactions

Being out and about can be a challenge, but social situations are valuable opportunities for your child. They enable him to broaden his communication and social skills as well as to be challenged to function with the rest of society.

After NICU

If your child's need was identified at birth, he may have been in the neonatal intensive care unit of a hospital for some time. Family and friends may have come to the hospital to show support, but until your baby came home, you and your spouse may have been the primary contacts with your baby as well as the obvious decision makers regarding his care.

Upon your baby's arrival home, family and friends will meet your baby. Before they may have helped with your other children and household tasks so that you could spend more time at the hospital; now they will have a greater opportunity to hold and care for your baby. Teach others how to help and include them in day-to-day routines when possible. The more you encourage and guide this interaction, the stronger their bond with your baby and the better their understanding of what is most helpful.

Struggles at School

Perhaps your child is just now beginning to struggle in school. If your child is tested for special services and begins to leave the "regular" classroom, other families will look to you for guidance in how to perceive your child.

 Question

How much should I share about my child's special needs?
Share information any time that your child's safety is involved. In other situations, the amount of confidential information that you share is a family decision. Certainly it is better for others to understand that your child has a special need (such as ADHD) than to think he is simply undisciplined.

Enjoy your child. Undoubtedly, your family has fun times at home where you enjoy and value each family member for who he or she is. Let that same acceptance and pride show at school. If your child does something funny (yet so kid-like) during the school music program, laugh. Smile. Others will learn to accept your child for the great person he is.

Respond to his needs. If your child does leave the "regular" classroom for some kind of special services, in a sense, that is no one else's business. It's also very possible that you'll want to share some of your feelings and concerns with certain friends or family members.

There is a fine line between guarding confidential information about your child and acting in a way that others will interpret as embarrassment about his needs. You do not want your child to adopt that outlook. Find the happy medium that works for your family.

Have You Noticed?—Reactions Near and Dear

Some people will question whether or not *you* have noticed your child's struggles. Just because you have not shared personal details with them does not, of course, mean that you have not realized your child's need.

Some reactions to your child's needs will strike a chord. Sometimes the comments, questions, suggestions, or looks are unintentional. Sometimes they are thoughtless or unaware. Seldom are reactions meant to be hurtful. Often comments and looks do hurt, though, regardless of the intent. Recognize that naturally you will feel for your child. Your best response is usually to be your child's best advocate and be positive and willing to teach others.

Family Gatherings

Family gatherings can be great for introducing your child to the world of "others." It is an opportunity for you to explain your child's needs and to team with others who want to help. Your extended family is one of the largest support groups your child will have outside of the special education team at school and certain special needs agencies and organizations.

Family Food

Food is often a central component at family gatherings. The hostess may make traditional (and perhaps costly) dishes for special get-togethers. Visiting family members may bring dishes to share. Although family favorites and comfort food may sound good to you, your child may not share your feelings. Some children have special food needs. Others are resistant to trying new foods because of taste, color, or texture.

 Alert

If your child has allergies or a special diet, share the information with family members who will be cooking ahead of time. Give them the opportunity to include your child's needs in the menu. If she needs a diet that is tough to follow or if the cook is concerned, assure her that you have the food covered.

Follow the share-a-dish plan. Bring one or several dishes that your child will eat. Your contribution to the meal can relieve stress for your child and your hostess.

Take some additional backup items just for your child that you are sure she will tolerate. This is especially important if you will be staying overnight with family. Also, have a quick-fix meal plan for your child that you can use after a trip to the store. Expanding food tolerance is important, but addressing it at Aunt Jane's house on Thanksgiving is not the best plan.

Family Activities

Think about the activities that happen at family get-togethers. Is your family generally active? Perhaps they are the type to play family football in the backyard. Maybe they are more subdued and tend to sit around the dining room table and chat. Have a plan for your child during these family activity times.

If your family is the active type, plan ways for your child to be involved. Can you or another family member be an assistant? Perhaps your child has a physical disability. Because of limited use of his hands and arms, he may use an electric wheelchair. If your family plays baseball, you can hit the ball and let your child "run" to base.

If your family gatherings are on the quieter side, take along things that your child can do with the other young family members. Board games, small dolls or trucks, and DVDs are a few ideas.

Questions and Comments

Your family knows you better than anyone else. What they may not know is your child's needs and how to be appropriately supportive and involved. Family members may seem to blurt out questions that are hurtful. They may seem to place blame for your child's condition. The comments may seem degrading toward your child or your efforts to be a good parent.

Remember that your family has not had the same experiences that you have had. You have learned about your child's specific needs. You are learning how to care for her and to have healthy expectations for her progress. Now you are also learning how to get your family members on board to motivate this wonderful, new family member.

Look for positives. When a family member interacts with your child, reinforce that interaction. Often people are afraid that they will do something wrong. Encourage interaction.

Follow up with supportive feedback. When Uncle Jim says, "Do you like football?" encourage your daughter to respond with her like or dislike of the sport. If she watches baseball without fail, make sure that Uncle Jim knows that so that the conversation continues.

Sometimes you may see or hear interaction that *is* degrading to your child. It is most likely unintentional, but you have an opportunity to steer things in the right direction. If Cousin Jeff comments on how your daughter (age sixteen) loves her toy car collection, chime in about the recent trip your daughter made to the community car show.

Enlisting Help

Getting your family involved in helping is another way to promote understanding. If you are the hostess preparing the family feast and it is time to feed your child, enlist a visiting family member. It is a perfect time for someone to help without fear of doing something wrong. You will be right there to offer on-the-spot guidance.

 Essential

You will be amazed at the reaction of family members who understand ways they can help. No doubt they have shared the same concerns and questions you had as you learned about your child's needs. The right information and something to do to help will make family members among your child's strongest advocates.

Do you need shirts that button down the front to accommodate your child's FM auditory trainer? Spread the word in the family. As others shop, they can be on the lookout for the needed items. It will save you time, and they will be pleased to help out.

Friends and Neighbors

Others around you will play an important role in your child's life. Friends and neighbors can offer a supportive network for your child to test his wings in communication and involvement outside of the family. Often in today's society we can get too busy to focus on time with friends and neighbors. Make time to be neighborly.

Help your friends and neighbors get to know your child. Explain his preferences, his needs, and the strategies that he uses instead of focusing on the disability per se.

Perhaps Justin is a ten-year-old with ADHD. You've decided that Justin will not take medication in the evenings, on weekends, and during the summer. He is very active (often impulsive) and apt to lose track of focus when doing chores and when it is time to come back in for supper. Try these prompts for addressing Justin's needs without going into all of the confidential information about his ADHD.

- "Justin needs to work off some extra energy so he is helping with the mulch. Isn't he doing a great job?"
- "Justin, I think you acted without thinking about the best choice. If Roger wants a turn on the trampoline, what could you do?"
- "Justin may come over to watch a movie. He loves to watch them so much. He may need a reminder to head back home when the movie is over."

Misunderstandings (about behaviors or needs) are the result of *not* understanding. Be on the lookout for ways to help others understand your child.

Restaurants

Going out to eat is common in today's fast-paced society where both parents often work outside of the home. The foods, environment, and social expectations of going to a restaurant should be considerations when choosing where to dine.

Foods

Does your child have a special diet? Some children with special needs have dietary needs. A few of the more common dietary restrictions include: no gluten, no caffeine, limited sugar intake, and no peanuts or their by-products.

Some children require foods that meet limited chewing and digestive abilities. Some children are resistant to eating foods that do not fall on a limited, preferred list.

Consider the foods offered by the restaurant. Are they ones that your child can tolerate health-wise? Are they foods that she is willing to eat? If the answer to either of those questions is no, your family has several choices:

- Choose another restaurant.
- Take alternate foods with you.
- Plan to eat at that restaurant at a future time without your child.

Environment

Consider the restaurant environment. Lights, noise, and too many people can make some restaurants overwhelming for a child on the autism spectrum. Some restaurants are more appealing at times other than the dinner rush. Tables that are too close together can make it uncomfortable and difficult for a child who uses a wheelchair or a walker.

Restaurant Behavior

Work with your child on appropriate restaurant behaviors. Staying at the table, using a quiet voice, not staring at others, and eating with generally good table manners are important. In order to help your child keep her behavior on track, try these ideas:

- Teach table manners at home.
- Talk about behavioral expectations *before* you go to the restaurant.
- Take a small activity bag with you to help your child as she waits for her meal. An activity bag might include paper and crayons, books, a small car or doll, or a small handheld game.

Most children with special needs easily pick up table manners if they are practiced at every meal, regardless of location.

Restaurant Workers

You will find most restaurant workers accommodating if they understand your needs (perhaps a table away from the busy center of the dining room) and if it is not their rush time of business. If your child has dietary considerations, call ahead and talk to the person in charge of the kitchen.

Other Diners

The other diners will be a contributing factor to the overall experience. In a close environment, people tend to stare, often without realizing it. Usually a firm, but definite, smile in their direction will remind them of their action. In general, think of the experience as a chance for others to see what a great child you have.

Stores

We live in a society that gets most items from stores. Food, clothing, entertainment, and transportation are all purchased. Having a child with a special need means purchasing some unique items (medical supplies, adapted clothing, study aids, dietary needs). It may mean additional shopping considerations as well (when, where, with whom).

Finding the Right Products

Finding products that fit the needs of your child might be tricky. Some children cannot eat foods with peanuts or their by-products. Having this allergy means more than just avoiding a PBJ sandwich. Some additives contain oils made from peanuts. Your weekly grocery shopping will take a little longer, at least until you learn which items are okay to toss in the cart. Extra shopping time may mean planning when you will shop with your child (when the store is less crowded or when your child is well rested). At times it might mean shopping without your child in tow.

Store Clerks

Clerks are similar to the waiters at the restaurant; most are helpful if they truly understand what you are asking. Perhaps you are shopping for color-coded school sets (red three-ring binder, red folder, red spiral notebook for Reading—the same items in blue for Math, etc.) to help your child stay organized at school. The store may have four color options (red, blue, green, and yellow). You may or may not choose to elaborate with the clerk why you need an orange set and a purple set as well.

If a particular store clerk is helpful and tries to locate the items you need, make a mental note. *That* is the store and the clerk to seek out with future shopping needs.

Other Shoppers

Other shoppers can be helpful (allowing you to go ahead of them in line), or they can obviously show pity in the manner of their actions and expressions (not so good). Yet other people may be unsure how to react and move away in awkward or fearful distance. Be thankful for the ones who treat you and your child like everyone else. Your positive attitude, ignoring inappropriate actions or looks, will serve as a model to other shoppers.

Store Behavior

Lighting, music, and other store features may actually be "stims" for your child. He may not be able to stop gazing at the lights. He may demand to use a particular door or to ride the escalator again and again. Some store behavior can be addressed before you go shopping. Explain: "We will ride up on the escalator one time. We will try on shirts for school. We will ride the escalator back down one time. Then we will come home."

Other Family Outings

The key to successful family outings is planning and a positive attitude. Plan everything that you can. Get information about the accessibility of your destination. If necessary, contact them ahead of time. Be aware of your food options. Take needed medication, equipment, and emergency contacts. When you have done everything you can do to plan for a smooth outing, relax. Unexpected things come up, but most often they are minor.

Theme Parks

There are several considerations when going to a theme park. If your child has a physical disability, contact the ride personnel for assistance in getting on and off the ride. Usually, you will not have to wait in the crowded wrap-around lines. There should be a separate gate to access most rides.

Make sure that your child has identification in case you are separated. If her condition affects her ability to communicate, include that information. (Perhaps she is deaf.) The identification should indicate if she is on any medication, in case of injury or unexpected illness. It is unlikely that you will be separated at all (if so, not for very long), but knowing that workers will be aware of your child's identification and immediate needs can be reassuring.

Find out where the park's medical office is located. This is helpful for situations other than emergencies. These might include special feeding arrangements (such as feeding through a G tube) and bathroom accommodations (if changing a diaper for a larger child).

Museums

Children's museums are popular destinations for families. Most offer engaging activities for kids, including hands-on displays and activities in which they can create related art projects.

Picking that all-important time when the museum is not too crowded and when your child is at her best is important. Contact the museum ahead of time for information on accessibility or if your child has communication needs (such as a sign language interpreter).

At the Zoo

Zoos offer a place for a leisurely stroll to see the animals, or activities for children and their parents. Before you head out to the zoo, make a list of each family member's priorities.

If your child adores monkeys, make sure that a stop to see the monkeys is high on the list. Include favorites for each family member. Remember that you are all part of the same family and respecting others' wants is an important trait for your child to learn.

 Fact

Watching animals is calming and entertaining for many children. Zoo animals can be viewed from afar. They don't require your child to interact as humans do through eye contact, speech, or close proximity. Household pets offer the same calming influence as well as unconditional love.

Movies and Other Productions

Children seem to be mesmerized by action on a movie screen, children's musical concerts, and most stage productions. Take care of physical needs (toilet, food, medications, and rest) beforehand. If your child needs an interpreter for the deaf or requires captioning, check ahead to find out the days and times those services are provided.

Office Visits and Other Appointments

You may feel like your appointment book is filled to the max. Necessary medical, dental, therapy, and educational appointments, in addition to other personal business appointments you may have, can consume a great deal of your time. An appointment time is perhaps the best time to make child care arrangements for all of your children. If that is not possible, choose your times carefully and go prepared with things for the children to do and appropriate snacks. A tired, hungry child is not a happy child—especially during an appointment.

Siblings' Office Visits

In a perfect world, you would take only one child to the doctor at a time. The others would stay with a family member or friend so that you could concentrate on the office visit without distractions. Of course, this is not a perfect world.

Try to plan office visits at a "good" time of the day. If your brood is ready to go first thing in the mornings, plan morning appointments. If everyone needs time to wake up, try to go later. Pack easy-to-take things to do and drinks and snacks for backup. Plan to do something special after the appointment that can be used as a behavior reward.

Rewards for "good" behavior do not have to be elaborate or expensive. You have already established a discipline and reward system (Chapter 7). Choose the type of reward that you are using with your child in other situations. For a child who is severely developmentally delayed, you may be using small food rewards throughout the visit. For other children, a preferred activity at a later time (time at the park, watching a favorite DVD, blowing bubbles in the yard) will be sufficient.

 **Alert**

Consistent expectations and follow-through are the best ways to get your children to do as you request. It is especially important that you are "a parent of your word" in appointment settings. Behavior rewards are for desired behavior. If your children are misbehaving, give a warning. If the behavior continues after a second warning, there is no reward.

School Meetings

As the parent of a child with special needs, you will have more school-related meetings than most parents. In addition to parent-teacher conferences with your child's inclusion teacher, you will meet with his special education teacher and possibly his therapists. Although they may meet with you as a group, the more people involved in the meeting, the longer the meeting will take. You may wish to ask for a longer appointment time to ensure that each participant will have time to present her information and suggestions. In many instances, it is easier to meet individually with those who work with your child.

In addition, the school will arrange an annual meeting to review your child's progress toward his educational goals, and to plan for his programming and goals for the following year.

School meetings are an important time to discuss your child's progress, to address any questions or concerns you have, and to see first-hand some of the materials used in the classroom. If possible, attend the meetings with your spouse and make arrangements for your children to stay with someone.

Parent Appointments

Child care (if available) also should be used for parent appointments. Trading child care with a neighbor or friend works for many families. As your child gets a little older, you may be able to trade child care with another family from his class. The time together can provide valuable social experience. You will be leaving your child with someone who understands his needs, and you will be able to take care of necessary business.

CHAPTER 11

The School Years

The initial realization that a child has a special need, the school years, and transition into adulthood are equally challenging stages of raising a child with a disability. Schools offer instruction in and assistance with a number of academic, social, and life skills. They also spark questions about the best way to educate a child. During the school years you will team with a number of professionals. You will be involved in the identification of your child's specific needs, and instrumental in planning how those needs are met.

School Struggles

You may have known, even before your child's birth, that she had special needs. You may not have had any concerns until it was time for her to walk or talk. Or you may not have realized that anything was amiss until the school years.

Preschool Screenings

School districts, in cooperation with regional special education programs, offer preschool screenings. Refer to Chapter 1 for more detailed information about preschool screenings. The importance of finding a disability and providing early intervention is critical to a child's success. However, not every special educational need can be caught in preschool screenings. It's impossible to assess a three-year-old's reading ability. It is also difficult to assess math computation in a child who is just learning to count.

Some children do not go through a preschool screening. They do not attend any kind of preschool or day care center that might pick up on the child's struggle. A red flag may not be raised until the child enters kindergarten and is introduced to schoolwork—reading, writing, and arithmetic.

Kindergarten

Kindergarten is considered by many to be the beginning of formal education. Whether your child attended an early childhood special education program, a traditional preschool, or did not go to any formal preschool program, you probably agree.

Many children with severe cognitive or developmental delays are not ready for the kind of kindergarten program that their peers will attend. Parents may assume that because their child has been working to get caught up for several years she has mastered the skills of "typically developing" children her age. However, she may or may not be ready to attend kindergarten in the "regular education" classroom. Some children, with the needed educational support, may be ready to learn with their peers. Others, however, need continued, intense special education—perhaps in the form of a transition kindergarten class or a specialized, self-contained program.

Some children may not have a known disability and first encounter educational difficulties in kindergarten. A child may have difficulty learning the letters of the alphabet and their sounds. She may not be able to rote count (counting just to count), and she may not be able to count a number of objects. Perhaps she cannot recognize printed numbers. Maybe just staying in her seat and listening to the teacher is difficult.

First Grade

In first grade, children are expected to take kindergarten skills to the next level. Although a child may have been taught a few sight words, first grade focuses on putting letter sounds together to read words. Most teachers believe that learning to read is the most important goal of first grade.

 Fact

Your child's school will conduct an annual hearing and vision screening for every student. If your child fails the screening, she may be retested on a later day. If she fails again, the school nurse will notify you that further testing by a doctor should be considered.

Math skills are taken to a higher level in first grade. Students are expected to add and subtract numbers. They begin to learn special math words that signal how to figure out simple word problems.

Third Grade

Third grade is another turning point in the school years. Incoming third graders are ready to take the basics of reading, writing, and arithmetic and use them to learn new information. Much of their earlier school years have focused on learning the skills. Now they are taking the skills and learning new concepts, such as science and social studies.

Fifth, Seventh, and Ninth Grade

Sometimes difficulties arise in the fifth, seventh, or ninth grades. These are often transition years when a child goes to a different type of school setup (where it's necessary to change classrooms, for example).

Some children with ADD or learning disabilities may have been successful in earlier years because of the supervision of one teacher. As expectations change and the student must keep herself organized, a previously undiagnosed problem can surface.

Request for Help

If you or your child's teacher is concerned about his ability to be successful in school, you may request help. That does not mean, however, that your child will receive special education services.

No Child Left Behind

With the recent legislation of No Child Left Behind, school districts are formalizing their efforts to help children succeed in the "regular classroom." In many districts, a team of professionals will discuss classroom concerns at the request of parents or the teacher. This team meeting can take place for a student of any age. The team may offer suggestions to your child's teacher. Perhaps an observation will be made of the overall classroom to offer additional ideas for the teacher to try in the classroom.

Response to Intervention

Schools are also establishing Reading Intervention programs (a part of RTI— Response to Intervention) for children who score significantly behind their peers in reading fluency and comprehension. This is based on screenings conducted with all students periodically throughout the school year. Children in Reading Intervention do not have IEP goals in Reading.

Observation

If you or your child's teacher has a concern, your child may be observed. Sometimes an observation of the entire class is done to offer instructional or classroom management ideas to the teacher. If your child is being evaluated for special education services, he may be observed in the classroom, on the playground, or even the lunchroom to see how he functions in school settings with his peers. Your child's teacher or the person heading up the evaluation will let you know that your child will be observed. She will not (for obvious reasons) explain to your child that someone wants to see how well he is doing.

Consultation

Your school's assistance team may suggest consultation from a professional in a specialized area to help your child and her teacher work better together. Consultation is used as a resource of ideas for classroom teachers and other school personnel. It is not a direct service to students.

When Consultation Is Used

A consultant may be called in to give input to a classroom teacher. For example, if a child's behavior is a cause for reoccurring concern in her third-grade classroom, a teacher of the behavior disordered or other behavioral specialist may be called in. Likewise, a preschooler may have difficulty with holding a crayon, cutting with scissors, and manipulating puzzle pieces. In this situation, an occupational therapist might be called for consultation.

A consultant's services may also be written into a child's IEP. Perhaps the child has difficulty with central auditory processing and uses an FM auditory trainer. Her IEP might include consultation for the classroom teacher on the use of the equipment as well as pointers for classroom instruction and management that will help the child succeed.

Consultation Providers

The professional providing consultation may be a staff member of the school district. This is often the case if services are needed from a professional commonly found in every school district—such as a school nurse. This is also the case in larger school districts that employ more specialized professionals—such as a physical therapist or an occupational therapist.

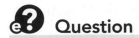 **Question**

Who pays for a consultant?
In general, a consultant is called into a classroom based on the concerns of school personnel. In this situation, the school district pays for the consultant unless, of course, the individual is a staff member. In some instances, only the family requests consultation. The responsibility of payment then depends on the unique situation.

The consultant might come from a regional special education program that serves a number of school districts. These programs offer services for less frequently occurring needs—such as teaching the visually impaired. Most school districts do not have enough blind children to warrant hiring such a specialist. They contract with a regional program for services as needed.

Referral for Special Education Evaluation

If your child is referred to the school's assistance team and the suggestions given to the classroom teacher do not take care of the concern, your child may be referred for a special education evaluation.

You will receive an "invitation" to a meeting to determine if a special education evaluation should be conducted. Besides you, the people at this meeting will include an administrator from your child's school, a school psychologist, your child's teacher, and a special education teacher.

The team will discuss your child's performance in the classroom and the specific concerns that brought about the meeting. The team will decide if an evaluation is needed and, if so, what types of testing should be done.

An evaluation may consist of observations, request of doctors' records regarding diagnosis of a disability, IQ and ability testing, and interviews with you, the teacher, and your child. A school district has sixty days to complete the evaluation. Another meeting will then be held to discuss their findings.

The IEP

When the school district contacts you for a meeting to discuss the findings of your child's evaluation, you must be given ten days' notice. You may waive your rights and have the meetings sooner at an agreed upon time. You will receive a packet or pamphlet that outlines your rights as parents.

 Fact

> Your child's school will report his progress on IEP goals in writing four times a year. One of these reports will be part of your child's annual review. Familiarize yourself with his goals and plan a regular time at home to practice them. The progress made on these goals will be one factor in writing his IEP for the next school year.

If your child's evaluation shows the need for special education services, you will work with the team to write an IEP. The IEP will document your child's level of functioning in academic, social, and behavioral areas. This document will also outline the special services, goals, modifications, adaptations, and testing procedures for your child. The IEP is a document that applies to the specified areas of your child's education.

Special Services

Special services will be listed on your child's IEP. It will specify the amount of time for each service, and if he will receive the services in the inclusion classroom, the special education classroom, a therapy room, or a combination of places.

If a professional is only providing consultation services, it will also be listed on the IEP. For example, a child who is blind may not need ongoing orientation and mobility training. He may, however, need direct services at the beginning of the year to learn his new surroundings and then need consultation services for the teacher at specified intervals throughout the year.

Goals

Your child's goals and objectives will be a major part of his IEP. These will list the things that will be included and monitored in your child's program to ensure that he is making progress.

Goals and objectives are based on state learning standards. They are written for those skills in which your child falls significantly behind. IEP goals and objectives do not include everything that will be studied. If your child is learning third-grade math, for example, he may have a goal to learn basic addition and subtraction facts because he has not had success in mastering them. But every third-grade math concept will not be listed as a goal or objective.

Modification and Accommodations

One section of your child's IEP will list agreed-upon modifications and accommodations. A few common modifications and accommodations on IEPs include:

- Shortened assignments or spelling lists
- Having tests (except for Reading tests) read to the child
- Use of a calculator
- Study guides for tests
- Preferential seating
- A note taker

The appropriate accommodations for your child will be decided at the IEP meeting.

Testing

Your child's IEP will designate *how* testing will take place. Some common testing accommodations include:

- Providing extended time to take the test
- Testing in a small group, such as in a special education classroom
- Having the test read to the student
- Allowing the student to use a calculator

 Alert

Your child's IEP cannot specify that a Reading test will be read to him. Reading tests are designed to do just that—test a child's ability to read. If a Reading test is read aloud to a student, the scores become an indication of how well the child listens rather than how well he reads.

Familiarize yourself and your child with the accommodations listed on the IEP. Teach your child to ask politely if accommodations are overlooked throughout the school day. Teachers are only human and can obviously make mistakes. Your child's teacher will be anxious to address the accommodations listed. Note that the accommodations your child needs, if any, will be applicable to standardized tests as well as regular tests given throughout the school year.

Annual Reviews

Once a year, your child's IEP will be reviewed. His current performance in academic and social/behavioral areas will be updated. So will his goals and objectives. At the annual review meeting, the team will talk about which subjects he will have in the inclusion classroom and which subjects he will attend in the special education classroom.

You do not have to wait until your child's annual review to have a meeting. If you have concerns, you may request a meeting at any time. Request a meeting by contacting your child's teacher or the special services office. The IEP is written to meet the needs of your child and can be changed if needed.

Re-evaluations

Every three years, your child's eligibility for special education is up for re-evaluation. In many instances, the team will decide that the child's current placement is working and that there has been no change in eligibility.

A child with a learning disability may be doing well in his current classroom placement. The team may agree that further evaluation is not needed. On the other hand, they might decide to test his reading skills because they are considering placing him back into the inclusion classroom for that subject.

504 Plans

Some children have a documented disability, but they do not need direct instruction from a special educator. For example, a child with ADD who is experiencing tremendous difficulty with organization may be receiving good grades regardless of the disability. A 504 plan can offer organizational assistance.

Paperwork

A team consisting of your child's teacher, a special educator, a school administrator, a representative from the special education administration, and yourself will write the 504 plan. It is a document that will stay with your child from year to year in order to provide consistent accommodations. The 504 plan will be reviewed on an annual basis and rewritten as needed.

Modifications and Accommodations

The 504 plan will spell out any special modifications or accommodations needed in your child's class. Common 504 accommodations and modifications include:

- Additional time to complete tests
- Assignment notebook check (to make sure that the work is listed fully and correctly)
- Periodic help/supervision to keep desk organized
- Consultation from appropriate professionals
- Shortened spelling list
- Assignments graded without points off for spelling errors

504 Plan Concerns

Your child's 504 plan will include a designated *case manager* who will be responsible for making sure that the plan is followed. If you have concerns about the 504 itself or if the school is not adhering to the document, you should contact the case manager. At any time you may also request a meeting with the 504 team to discuss the document.

 Essential

There may be times in your child's school career when she will need an advocate. An advocate is someone who offers ideas and support, or goes to bat for someone else. That role will be held by many different people in the course of your child's life. Sometimes the advocate is your child's best friend. Sometimes it might be a lawyer. Read more about advocacy in Chapter 21.

IDEA

The Individuals with Disabilities Education Act (IDEA) is legislation that provides for special education for children with disabilities. Originally it was written in 1997 and reauthorized in 2004. With the reauthorization came some changes in the identification of children with special needs, delivery of services, qualification of special education teachers, and evaluation guidelines. To learn more about IDEA 2004, refer to the resources cited in Appendix A.

Communication

Keep the communication lines open with the professionals who work with your child. As he gets older, the type or frequency of the communication may change, and more of the responsibility will fall onto your child's shoulders.

School-Home Notebooks

Purchase a spiral notebook at the beginning of the school year. On the inside cover, write your phone number with a message to call if the notebook is found. In order to protect your child's confidential information, it is not necessary to write his name.

The notebook will travel back and forth between home and school daily in your child's backpack. Make entries for important information for the teacher regarding things such as appointments requiring your child to miss school, events at home such as a relative visiting or a sibling's birthday, and if your child did not sleep well the previous evening. If it is something that will affect your child's day at school, it should go into the notebook. The home-school notebook works well with young students who have difficulty explaining changes to their teacher. In the same manner, the teacher will note events, successes, and concerns of the school day.

Assignment Notebooks

When your child reaches third or fourth grade, he is ready to keep an assignment notebook. This is a great way to keep track of the required homework and upcoming activities at school.

As your child maintains his assignment notebook, he is learning responsibility and to ask questions regarding things that he does not understand. Some children need a teacher to check over the homework entries and help them gather their homework materials before leaving school.

Phone Calls

Phone calls offer a personable way to communicate with the school staff members. It is faster to make a phone call than write a lengthy note when you have multiple items to discuss.

Even so, phone calls are not always the best choice. You do not know if you are calling at a bad time. Also, you do not have a written record of what was discussed for your reference. Sometimes it is tricky remembering important details unless they're in writing. For example, which day will the physical therapist observe your child in the classroom?

E-mail

E-mail seems to be the current communication of choice. An e-mail can be read at the recipient's convenience, but sometimes will be read and responded to immediately. E-mail also provides the needed text for later reference. It can be easy to misplace a slip of paper, but it's pretty hard to lose a computer!

Conferences

Sometimes it is necessary to have a conference. You may wish to have a conference when multiple people need to be involved. This may be the case if your child has more than one teacher. Conferences can be held during formal parent-teacher conference dates or more informally at your request. Remember that you can request that the IEP team meet any time you have concerns.

Medication Considerations

The question of medication will come up sooner or later. Some children obviously need medication for health reasons. For other children, the answer may be unclear. This is usually the case when considering medication to help a child focus on schoolwork or keep behavior in check.

 Alert

Tell your child's teacher when there are changes in medication (or if you run out). Otherwise she may dismiss some valuable observations, such as: your child is just tired, perhaps not feeling well, or being willfully difficult. Don't opt to "see if she notices a difference."

Consider the following questions and talk with your child's doctor as you make any choices regarding medication:

- What are the benefits of this medication?
- What are the possible side effects?
- When and where is paying attention most difficult?
- Is your child able to function successfully using strategies only?

Only you and the doctor can make the right medication choice for your child.

CHAPTER 12

School Strategies

The school years present a number of challenges for the child with special needs. According your child's IEP or 504 plan, he will have the opportunity to learn to his fullest potential, and will receive necessary modifications and accommodations. Know the expectations for all students and work to understand why these tasks are difficult for your child. Be ready to go with these school success strategies.

Know the Expectations

Even though many school districts strive for uniformity from class to class in a given grade level, each teacher has unique ways of doing things. Get an idea of what each teacher is looking for by reading (and saving) the handouts from the beginning of the year. Newsletters, assignment notebooks, and project information sheets are also important.

Class Routines

Each teacher has a pattern or routine for handling class work and discipline. Spelling sentences might always be due on Tuesdays. Maybe time is always given at the end of a class for students to begin on homework and to ask for help. Perhaps homework is turned in to a particular bin.

Find out what your child's teacher will grade and how it will be graded. Does spelling count? Does all work have to be shown for math problems? What kind of paper should be used? Are students allowed to use pens? Some of these things may seem picky, but they define the organization of the classroom. Unless something is included in the student's IEP or 504 plan as a modification or accommodation, it is good practice to follow the requirements of the class.

Be familiar with the behavior expectations of the classroom as well as the discipline procedures. Talk with your child about the expectations. A clear understanding before going into the situation will help her be more successful in following the rules.

Modifications and Accommodations

There are exceptions to classroom routines and rules. If the child's special need has an adverse effect on her schoolwork, she will likely have an IEP or a 504 plan. Either of these documents will spell out agreed-upon modifications and accommodations for schoolwork.

A student with a learning disability may need a shortened assignment in math or fewer spelling words. Perhaps the IEP or 504 plan specifies that tests (except for Reading tests) will be read to the student. Often children with behavior disorders have very specific behavior plans (including incentives and consequences). Modifications and accommodations are decided by the parents, a team of school professionals, and the child herself if she is old enough.

Have a Schedule

Homework is a part of every student's life regardless of special need. This is true for the preschool child who is working on speech words; it is true for the high school student with a learning disability who is approaching final exams. Your family may have many obligations, including sports, clubs, and community activities. Perhaps you have more than one child. Create a homework schedule to help your entire family understand the importance of homework in your child's learning. Just as a soccer team has designated times to practice and specific things to do, so it is with the child with special needs and schoolwork.

Routine Homework

Some assignments are routine. Your child's teacher may ask that students turn in vocabulary definitions every Wednesday. Because this is a routine assignment, you can space out the needed work. By dividing the list of words over several days, your child can meet the Wednesday due date and yet have enough time to complete unexpected assignments.

Unexpected Assignments

Every classroom has some assignments that are not routine. The moment that you read your child's assignment notebook may be the first time you know that there are two math worksheets for homework. Make sure your child's homework schedule includes time for unexpected work.

Big Projects

Big projects should be scheduled over time. Guide your child in choosing a project that is challenging but doable. A child with a hearing loss may have difficulty writing lengthy reports, so a photo essay with captions would be a much better match for the child's visual focus.

Working on Needed Skills

Basic school skills such as reading sight words and remembering math facts can be a struggle. Plan a regular time to work with the child on these skills. Keep three things in mind when working on these skills:

- Make sure that the material is at an appropriate level.
- Plan a small amount of time to practice on a regular basis.
- Vary the way the practice is done by using a variety of materials: flashcards, games, worksheets, computer activities.

The key to a successful homework schedule is to have a realistic plan that you follow consistently.

Math Facts

Whether balancing a checkbook or following a recipe, math facts are a part of life. Calculators offer help, but a basic knowledge of math is as important as knowing how to read. Without it, life success will be compromised.

Breaking Down the Facts

First, choose the operation (addition, subtraction, multiplication, or division). Talk to your child's teacher to help you decide where to begin. Even though your daughter is in the fifth grade, she may not have mastered the addition facts.

 Essential

An accommodation can help a child who is having difficulty remembering the facts, but is ready for more difficult math concepts. A fifth grader may struggle to remember multiplication facts, but she may understand that the area of a rectangle is found by multiplying length by width. Her IEP might include an accommodation to use a calculator or multiplication chart.

Next, plan which facts to study. Quizzing your child on all of the addition facts to start with can be overwhelming. Begin with all the "plus one" facts (2+1, 3+1, 4+1, etc.). When your child masters those, practice the "plus two" facts. Then practice both sets together. Continue to include the next group of facts. This will take time.

Remembering Math Facts

A child with a learning disability can take a long time to master math facts. Truthfully, some children may never memorize them. Others (such as some children with Asperger's syndrome) may memorize them with little effort. Still others will memorize them by learning them in a song. Learning math facts happens over time. Patience, persistence, and a plan to study the facts in order are key.

Math Word Problems

Generations of students have hated math word problems. They can be especially tricky for your child for four reasons.

1. Word problems require reading.
2. Word problems have key words that tell which operation to use.
3. Many word problems involve multiple steps (requiring the solution of more than one problem to get the final answer).
4. Word problems use math facts for computation.

If your child has a great deal of difficult reading word problems in math, read them out loud while he follows along.

Recognizing Math Words

Have your child circle the words that tell which operation to use. Make a list of these words for your child to use later.

ADDITION WORDS

- In all
- The sum of
- All together
- The total

SUBTRACTION WORDS

- How many more
- How many less
- The difference
- How many left

Before he begins his homework, review the math words and which operation they represent.

Follow the Example

In general, children avoid math book examples. This is especially true of many children with learning disabilities. The wording with the examples is often confusing and difficult to read.

 Fact

Children with ADD or ADHD can be frustrated with the steps involved in math. They often just want to get the work done. Break an assignment into smaller parts (only a few problems at a time) to keep your child focused. Switch to another assignment or take a break before starting the next set of problems.

The examples are obviously there for a reason. When he is stuck, have your child look over the examples (disregarding the words). Have him follow the steps or pattern to complete similar problems.

Read, Draw, Reread, Compute, Reread, Check

Ask your child to read the problem aloud. (Or read the problem as your child follows along.) Reread it, stopping at the first point that requires action. Here is an example:

Mary plants a garden that is in the shape of a rectangle.

1. Stop and have your child draw a rectangle to represent the garden.

It is 10 feet long and 5 feet wide.

2. Stop and have your child label the sides of the garden.

How many feet of fencing in all will she need to go around the entire garden?

3. Ask your child to identify the key math words *in all*. Ask which operation the words represent—addition.
4. Have your child compute the answer. What is the problem asking? Add a label word—*feet*.
5. Reread the entire problem. Have him check his work.

Following all of the steps, showing the work, adding a label, and checking for math errors are all important tasks.

Spelling Words

Spelling skills are critical for more than just spelling class. Knowing how to spell words in writing is also important.

Sizing Up the List

Help your child identify spelling patterns (*at, bat, cat, fat, mat, sat, rat*). These are easier than the vocabulary-spelling words from the week's reading story that often come in older grades.

With vocabulary spelling words, have your child look for smaller words within the word (*math* and *mat* are in *mathematical*) or listen for familiar sound patterns.

Accommodations and Modifications

Again, accommodations and modifications are listed on a child's IEP or 504 plan. Some common modifications for spelling tests are to give a shortened list or to concentrate on words that follow a particular spelling pattern instead of a vocabulary-based word list.

Ways to Practice

Spelling words may be practiced orally, by writing the words, typing them on the computer, filling in missing letters, and arranging tiles with letters. Some children need to have the tactile experience of arranging plastic letter tiles. Others learn better by hearing and reciting the spelling.

 Question

Why does my child do well on spelling tests but can't spell the same words correctly in her written work?
Often test material is learned for the moment. Your child may not yet have automatic recall of the word. She may be concentrating on other rules of writing (such as beginning a sentence with a capital letter).

Practice can be done in any way that is helpful, but it is wise to include the way in which your child will be tested. For example, if she will have to write the words for testing, have her write the words as you dictate them.

Beyond the Test

Help your child create two spelling word reference lists to use in her future writing. This can be done with a spiral notebook. First, print one letter of the alphabet at the top of each page, counting the front and back of a sheet as one page. Spelling words may be added to this list for her to use as a reference. Further back in the notebook print a spelling pattern at the top of each sheet (*at, in, ale, ean,* etc.). Some words will be on both lists.

Reading

Reading is important for everyday life skills such as getting a job and simply understanding a bus schedule. Reading is also a wonderful form of entertainment. Take time to work with your child on building strong reading skills. Don't forget to let him see you enjoying a good book.

Sight Words

One of the first steps in reading is learning what teachers call *sight words*. Sight words are words that are frequently seen in reading material. They are often (but not always) short. Sight words do not follow a specific spelling pattern like *it, bit, fit, hit, pit,* and *sit.* Children must either learn to sound out the word, or to simply memorize them.

School districts begin to teach and evaluate children on sight words in kindergarten. Depending on the school district, children are responsible for twenty to thirty of these words. Check with your child's teacher to see which ones are currently being taught at school.

Learning to Read

Once a child has mastered a number of basic sight words, he is ready for stories with short sentences. Often these stories follow a pattern:

The boy ran to the tree.

The boy ran to the wagon.

The boy ran to the fence.

The boy ran to the mailbox.

The boy ran and ran and ran.

Do not be worried that your child is only memorizing the word pattern. This kind of repetition and tackling the different words at the end of each sentence is a typical beginning reading skill.

Reading for Fun

As your child learns to read, he will have several levels of reading skills. You can help foster his enjoyment of reading by:

- Choosing some books for him to read for fun. The words should be mostly ones that he can read without difficulty.
- Choosing some books to read together. Take turns reading the pages in a book.
- Choosing some books that are too hard for your child to read. Read these out loud to encourage your child to build his reading skills. There are lots of great books out there!

Textbook Tips

Many children with special needs are overwhelmed by textbooks. Reading is often difficult for them, and textbooks challenge them with new ideas as well as with the need to use reading skills. In addition, it is common practice to place children in inclusion classrooms for some combination of math, science, and social studies as first experiences. These classes require textbook reading.

Preview/Review

Beat the homework/study game by helping your child preview a new lesson or chapter. Look at the pictures and talk about what your child thinks is happening. Read the captions and talk about the tables. Read the titles and headings. Read the differently colored vocabulary words. Read the summary and the questions at the end of the passage.

Headings and Vocabulary

Explain to your child that book makers want them to know the important words and ideas. Show your child the titles and headings in a lesson. Explain that these help people know *where* to look for answers. Talk about the vocabulary words (usually in boldface or a colored font). Explain that these are often, but not always, the answers to questions.

Review Material

After your child has a lesson at school, reread the material at home. Try this if your child has reading skills below grade level. Have her listen as you read a paragraph, and then have her retell the important information. Again, the headings and colored or bold print should be reviewed.

Auditory Learning

Children with auditory processing problems and those with below-grade level reading skills may benefit from listening to audio recordings of a textbook. Audio versions of many textbooks (often playable at only one speed) are available from publishers. Specially formatted audio books are available free of charge to qualifying students from Recording for the Blind and Dyslexic. Using specially designed audio equipment or related computer software, these CDs can be played at various speeds. Dyslexic students may follow along in the book.

Test Preparation

Teachers give different kinds of tests. Some are simply a list of vocabulary words and their definitions. Others are multiple choice covering one or more chapters. Still others require a written essay on a topic. Most teachers give a particular range of test types (for example, always a vocabulary quiz followed by a multiple-choice chapter test, or only essay tests). It is critical for you and your child to know what kind of test will be given.

Study Guides and Practice Tests

Every parent can relate to studying for the wrong kind of test or studying the wrong information. Know what material your child's teacher recommends for study. Is there a practice test at the end of the chapter? Does the teacher give a study guide with key points? Explain to your child the kind of questions that will be included.

Flashcards

Flashcards can be made from a variety of materials: construction paper, card stock, and index cards. It is important that the cards be durable enough to withstand the amount of handling needed for practice, and that the answers cannot be read from the other side of the card. One side of each card should have a single question or definition; the answer goes on the other side.

Flashcards permit you to single out the information that needs more practice. For example, out of twenty-five cards, the child may be able to answer fifteen readily. Place those in a separate pile to be reviewed several times before the test. Have your child practice more with the remaining difficult questions.

 **Question**

Should children make their own flashcards?
This depends on the maturity, attention, and fine motor skills of the child. Make cards for your child while he is young. When he reaches upper elementary, junior high, and high school, have him make at least some of the needed cards.

Flashcards work especially well with children who have attention difficulties. They are able to focus on a single question; they also are encouraged as the "mastered" pile grows.

Understanding Test Words

Recognizing important words in questions is necessary to choose or write a correct response. If a question asks: "Who was the first president of the United States?" the key words are *who, first, president,* and *United States.* Negatives are especially tricky. For example:

1. Which is not a season?
   a. summer
   b. rain
   c. spring

Explain the question says *not.* Then ask your child to identify the correct sentence: "Rain is *not* a season."

Setting a Pace

Studying for a test falls under the "big project" category. The night before the test is too late to start. If the teacher gives a science vocabulary quiz for every chapter, tackle it as a big project. Chances are that she explains a few of those words with each lesson. As she does so, add those flashcards to the stack to be studied. Develop a homework routine that includes five or ten minutes for this each evening. Watch your child's self-esteem rise with his grades!

Writing

A child with special needs may have difficulty writing for a number of reasons. She may have trouble putting her thoughts in words or elaborating on one basic idea. Focusing on what to say often results in her forgetting capitalization and end punctuation. Because spelling does not come easily, the entire task may seem like torture.

Writing a Sentence

Start with small steps to help your child with sentence writing. In fact, first encourage her to write single words. Go on to short phrases, then tackle sentences.

CHECKLIST FOR A GREAT SENTENCE

✓ Start with a capital.
✓ Use a capital for names of people, places, and things.
✓ Write a complete idea.
✓ End with a punctuation mark.

Have your child make a book based on a fun experience, such as going to the zoo. Have her illustrate four or five things she saw or did, then have her write a sentence for each one.

Writing a Paragraph

Children are ready to write paragraphs *only* after they become proficient with sentences. Have your child use a graph like the one below to help her organize her thoughts before she begins a paragraph.

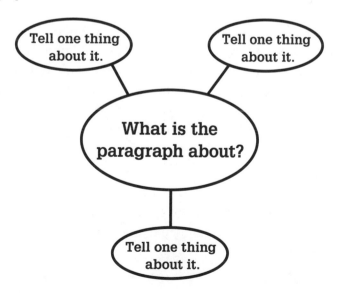

Have your child use the sentence checklist with the paragraph checklist below. In a sense, writing a paragraph is similar to working a math word problem. Follow the steps and check your work to get a good product.

CHECKLIST FOR A GREAT PARAGRAPH

✓ Write a sentence to tell what the paragraph is about.

✓ Write three more sentences. Each sentence should tell a detail.

✓ Write a sentence to tell what the whole paragraph is about.

✓ Check each sentence for capitals and end punctuation, and make sure it's a complete thought. Use the sentence checklist.

Writing a paragraph will call for more supervision and more encouragement than completing a homework worksheet. Redirect your child to the checklists, give lots of positive feedback, but try to resist leading her through the work. It is important that she develop her own writing skills without depending on continual monitoring.

Writing an Essay

It can be a long road from writing a few letters of the alphabet to some kind of essay composition. Most children with special needs can reach this goal *if* they use the necessary tools. Remember that writing skills are acquired gradually over time.

THE ORDER OF WRITING SKILLS

1. Single letters of the alphabet
2. Words
3. Phrases
4. Sentences
5. Paragraphs
6. Essays

Have your child plan the paragraphs for an essay using a more elaborate graphic organizer than for a paragraph.

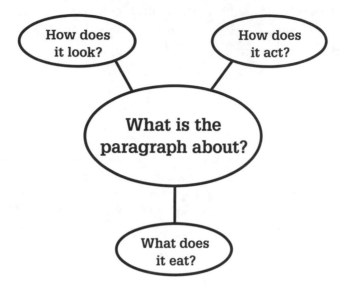

Beginning essays usually include an introduction paragraph, three body paragraphs, and a conclusion paragraph. Using the paragraph-writing graph, have your child describe an animal. Have her write three body paragraphs, including: three things the animal eats; three details about its appearance; and three details about how it acts. Creating a paragraph for each of the sets of smaller details is a great way to write the body of the essay.

Tutors

A parent, other family member, friend, high school or college student, teacher, or professional tutor may be a good tutor for a child with special needs. Anyone who understands how your child learns and the material that he needs to learn can be a tutor. It sounds simple, but finding a good tutor can be tricky.

Cautions

Some well-meaning tutors may feel sorry for a child with special needs. Empathy is one thing, but pity on the part of a tutor will result in your child learning excuses for why he cannot do something, instead of making progress to his fullest ability.

 Alert

When talking to a prospective tutor for your child, discuss what will be covered. Will the tutor follow your child's textbook, or will he be using other, similar materials? Using the child's textbook can be helpful as long as the tutor makes sure that your child understands the concepts but does his own work.

Other tutors may fully understand how the special needs of your child affects his learning. They may not, however, understand what your child's peers are learning or the steps in learning to get to that material. For example, a tutor may well understand that some students with learning disabilities seem to "have" a concept one day and seem to have never seen the material the next day. That same tutor, however, may not have a clear concept of the methods used to teach multiplication to third graders and the level of difficulty presented in that grade.

Benefits

Regardless of the considerations in getting a tutor, they can offer many benefits. Sometimes your child may need to hear his school subjects explained in a different way or from someone other than a family member.

Some families find that tutoring is beneficial during the summer months. Children have the opportunity to catch up on skills when they don't have to be concerned about homework.

CHAPTER 13

Gadgets and Gizmos

People are intrigued with gadgets. They can make life easier and more interesting. Entire stores are geared toward gadgets, gizmos, and technology wonders. Many provide a useful purpose. Some are just for fun. Children with special needs can often benefit from carefully chosen gadgets and gizmos. Often a little device can provide the assistance needed for a child to complete a task independently or to participate in recreational fun. Be on the lookout for gadgets and gizmos that will work for your child.

Getting Around

Some devices for children with special needs are no-nonsense equipment prescribed by a physician or therapist. Many of these items are used by children with low vision, blindness, or a physical disability. Braces, crutches, and walkers are a few of the orthopedic aids used by children and teens with a physical need. These are specially prescribed items based on the needs of the individual.

Wheelchairs are used by children who cannot walk or have difficulty standing and walking for any distance. There are two main types of wheelchairs: manually operated and electric. Electric wheelchairs run on the power of a large battery that is charged when not in use. Some wheelchairs can be folded up to transport more easily in a car or van. Others (including the electric wheelchairs) have a fixed position and cannot be folded.

A child or teen who is blind may be instructed in the use of a cane by an orientation and mobility teacher. Kiddie canes might be considered first canes for young children. Their design includes a wrist band and groove to help the child with finger placement. In addition, the round tip, light weight, and smaller size are ideal for beginning users. Various pre-canes and adapted canes are also available to meet individual needs of older children.

Teens with low vision are sometimes able to drive with special mirrors to compensate for their visual acuity or range of vision. Teens with limited use of their legs may benefit from hand controls for braking and acceleration. Some use a spinner knob to help in turning the steering wheel.

 Fact

The Association for Driver Rehabilitation Specialists (also called ADED, the Association of Driver Educators of the Disabled) includes professionals who provide driver education and evaluation of a driver's special needs, including adaptive car equipment, as well as those who sell those devices. The ADED also offers a program that certifies instructors who are called Certified Driver Rehabilitation Specialists (CDRS).

Communication

Perhaps one of the most important functions of technology is assistance with communication. Enabling a child to express his wants and needs is critical to his physical and emotional well-being. A number of devices are available to meet individual communication needs.

FM Auditory Trainers

Children who are deaf or have significant hearing loss may use an FM auditory trainer in school. A microphone is worn by the teacher or speaker, and a receiver is worn by the student. Some receivers are worn behind the ear and others consist of a small box worn on the chest with a harness, connected with cords to a piece that fits into the student's ear.

 Alert

A speaker who is wearing an FM auditory trainer microphone should be aware that it will amplify her voice even when she is not in the same room with the student. A conversation in the hall with another teacher or noise from the bathroom can be sent to the student's "receiver" if the microphone is not turned off.

An FM auditory trainer has several settings. It can be used as a powerful hearing aid that amplifies all the voices and other sounds in the room, or it can be used to focus primarily on the speaker's voice. As the speaker's voice is picked up by the microphone, it is channeled to the receiver, minimizing other sounds in the room. With less input from background noise, the child is better able to focus on and understand the speaker's speech.

Communication Boards

Some children on the autism spectrum or with physical impairments that affect speech benefit from communication boards. This type of assistive technology is often called *augmentative communication*. A variety of types is commercially available. Using augmentative communication, the child points to a picture or symbol on a "board" and the product will then speak the desired word or phrase. Some are preprogrammed with words; in other products, a specific message can be recorded to correspond with each picture.

Augmentative devices can be as simple as two to four pictures, or they may use a large number of picture or icon choices.

Head Wand

Head wands are used by some children with severe physical disabilities. The child wears a headband that supports the wand, which is used to point to a place on a communication board or on a computer screen. The equipment then "speaks" for the child.

Communication Book

A child with a severe communication delay might use a picture system, called *The Picture Exchange Communication System* (PECS), to communicate wants and needs. This is often used by children on the autism spectrum who struggle with verbal language. In this system, the child chooses a small picture card to ask for something, or to answer a question. PECS was created by Andrew Bondy, PhD, and Lori Frost, MS, CCC/SLP.

Gadgets and Gizmos for Daily Living

Assistive devices are important for mobility and education. They are also important for the day-to-day functioning of your child. Independence is the goal; with independence comes increased self-esteem.

Daily Living Help for the Deaf

A child with a hearing impairment will probably use amplification to get the most benefit from her residual hearing. She will also use vision or feeling (vibration) for assistance in daily tasks. The phone and the doorbell can be hooked up so that a light flashes in addition to the customary sound. Special alarm clocks also flash a light. Some can be connected to the bed so that the bed vibrates when the alarm goes off.

"Phone calls" are made through a TDD (telecommunications device for the deaf)—often called a TTY (teletypewriter). Frequently, however, a computer program is used that allows the participants to see each other on the screen and communicate through sign language.

 Fact

The Telecommunications Act ensures that equipment will be available from manufacturers that allows individuals with communication difficulties (such as the hearing impaired) to communicate with others. Telephone relay services are included in this act as well as the closed captioning provided on television and in recent educational films. All televisions manufactured since 1994 have closed captioning display capabilities.

Other individuals who have a hearing loss communicate through a voice carry over (VCO) system. In this system, a person who is hearing impaired communicates with a hearing person by calling a relay center. She types her messages through a computer or TTY. The relay operator "voices" the message to the hearing person. When the hearing person responds, he types the message and sends it to the person who is hearing impaired.

Assistive Devices for the Blind

Children who have low vision, or who are blind, learn to use sound or synthetic voice equipment to compensate. Some sound/ talking gadgets are watches, clocks, calendars, calculators, and money identifiers.

Other gadgets that do not make sounds are also available. Magnifiers (up to 30x), raised-ine paper, writing guides, enlarged numbered dials, the stylus used for Braille writing, and the Braille typewriter are examples. In addition, Braille label makers assist families in creating stick-on labels to mark items that cannot be distinguished by touch (spices, medicines, colors of paint, and games).

Daily Living Aids for the Physically Disabled

Gadgets and gizmos to assist with hygiene and dressing include a variety of bathing chairs, long-handled combs and brushes, zipper grips, and button hooks. Adapted utensils, cups, and dishes are available for dining. Around the home, your child may use a "reacher," a device that will help her grab a needed object that is beyond her range of motion.

Helpful Items for Children with Attention Difficulties

A watch with an easy-set alarm can aid the child or teen with attention difficulties to help her "remember" where she should be: home for dinner, at the door of the mall, leaving a friend's house. A small timer can also help to manage schoolwork and home chores. Perhaps fifteen minutes of practicing math facts is part of the homework routine. A timer can help your child stick with it.

CDs and Auditory Materials

Many children with special needs are auditory learners. Some are auditory learners because it is a natural aptitude, while others rely on auditory learning because they struggle with reading or have difficulty with visual acuity or visual perception. Some are auditory learners due to low vision or blindness.

Books on tape are available from Recordings for the Blind and Dyslexic (see Chapter 12) to assist students who have difficulty reading or seeing print materials. Some textbook companies also produce audio tapes. Even books for very young children with a picture sound strip help the reader associate the text with specific vocabulary or environmental sounds.

Music CDs offer another way to practice math facts and other rote memory information such as the months, days of the week, counting, the alphabet, and states and capitals. The material might be presented with a song, with rap music, or in chants and rhymes. These kinds of CDs are readily available through education catalogs or from teacher supply stores. When considering which ones to buy, check with your child's teacher for ones that are used at school and may be favorites. Also, consult the employees at the teacher supply store. They are often teachers, and can give you information on which ones address appropriate skills and are the most popular.

Other gadgets "talk" as well. Teens with a learning disability might benefit from some of the same gadgets used by a teen with low vision or blindness: a talking calculator, watch, scales, or thermometer.

Computer Programs

This is an age of computers. Computers are used in homes, in schools, and in businesses. Software programs are available for even very young babies. Many aspects of computer use are advantageous to the child with a special need. He will benefit from developing a range of strategies to use computers and related programs and devices to their fullest potential.

Spell Check

The spell check feature on computers is great—to a limited extent. If the writer meant to type *The boy ate hamburgers,* but typed *The boy are hamburger,* the spell check would miss the two incorrect words (*are* and *hamburger*). Although those words were not intended, they were indeed spelled correctly. For the student with a learning disability the spell check feature is helpful but cannot be used exclusively.

Skills Practice Programs

Your child can practice many skills with online skills practice programs or skills practice software. Computer activities and games are available for math, reading, spelling, writing and grammar, science, and social studies.

 Alert

Be picky about the computer practice programs that you let your child use. A program that promises addition practice may or may not be what your child needs. If he is learning math facts and the program asks him to add numbers in the hundreds, it is not a good match.

Check with your child's teacher about recommended computer programs. Often a list of Internet sites will be listed on a school website for at-home practice. Also, look up the publishers of the textbooks your child uses at school. Many have online practice activities that specifically go with the lessons or chapters in the book.

Visit a teacher supply store and talk with the employees about appropriate programs. Many stores are manned by certified teachers who can help you find the needed programs. Some stores have demo programs for you to see exactly what is included.

Screen Readers

Various software programs are on the market that will read aloud the information on a computer screen. Some programs "read" material from books and papers that have been scanned into the computer. Screen reading programs allow the student who has a reading disability or visual impairment to access print material for textbook assignments and research.

More Assistive Technology

Other assistive technology is available that works with, or in a similar fashion to, computers. Not all assistive technology is right for an individual within a particular area of special need. Work with the staff at your child's school or a representative from a supply company to try out and assess whether or not an item will work before making an expensive purchase.

Wireless keyboards are available for students with learning disabilities and those with minimal handwriting difficulty. The keyboards allow students to input notes, written assignments, or spelling test answers that can later be printed through a computer. For some students, a wireless keyboard offers a way to keep up with the physical requirements of writing for a class. Others find the smaller display screen difficult to use and prefer to use a laptop, computer terminal, or other arrangement.

Some children and teens benefit from auditory input. Reading a textbook or shuffling through notes and informational handouts can be overwhelming. Recording a lesson or lecture can be helpful so that the student can replay it later. However, listening to the recording is time-consuming, and it's difficult to find a particular place in the lecture.

Several types of electronic pens are available to assist the older student with a reading or learning disability. One kind will "read" the words on a page, functioning as a hand-held scanner. This kind of pen will also define a word that is targeted on the page of print. Another kind of pen will record the words of a speaker while being used to take notes. The notes can later be sent to a computer and accessed and searched for key words just like a computer document. The success of using either of these pens depends on the student's maturity and fine motor skills.

Sensory Integration

A child who is seeking sensory input in the classroom can be distracted from the schoolwork at hand. Her inability to stay on task can be problematic to students around her as well. Often, this problem can be alleviated by using small sensory items in therapy and in the classroom.

Tactile Items

Velcro can be used for tactile input when fidgety fingers are looking for something to do. Applying a strip of the self-stick Velcro under the child's desk provides an instant source of tactile input. The child can run her fingers along the strip as she listens to classroom presentations.

 Alert

"Squeeze" items are not right for every child. If your child bites or picks on things, consider whether the sensory item is safe for her. Some items are not manufactured for therapeutic use. Check occupational and speech therapy sites for specially made products.

Squeeze balls also provide sensory input. Many varieties are available commercially. Some are filled with clear water. Some have glitter or tiny floating objects inside. Others (made in different, themed shapes) are made of a squeezable foam material. Again, the child can squeeze the item for needed sensory input.

You can make your own squeeze ball at home. Put a small amount (¼–½ cup) of flour, sugar, or sand into a balloon. Secure it by tying the balloon closed. Again, consider whether this is appropriate and safe for your own child. Biting, picking, and latex allergies are a few considerations.

Some children with sensory integration difficulties crave deep pressure. This is sometimes treated with a special brushing program that involves repeated movements on the arms and legs using a surgical brush. This kind of program should be set up and monitored by an occupational therapist or doctor.

For some children, beanbag chairs are effective for providing deep pressure. As the child sits in the bean bag chair, she feels the comfort of the chair's snugness. Specially designed weighted vests and blankets can also be used for specified periods of time. As with all sensory input programs, these should be monitored by a trained therapist or doctor.

Seat cushions help some children stay focused at school. The cushions come in circle and wedge shapes and can be filled with air or liquid. The movement of the cushion requires the child to concentrate—on staying seated and on her work.

More School Helps

Other gadgets are helpful to students and, if appropriate, may be written into your child's IEP. Your child's teacher, therapists, and other school staff can teach your child how and when to use them. Some gadgets may be needed in all situations (raised-line paper might be used for a student with low vision). Other gadgets (such as calculators) should be used only in certain situations.

 Alert

Finding the right assistive technology for your child can take time, effort, and lots of patience. The key is to use technology that is a "good fit" for your child's needs. Sometimes children develop strategies that serve them better than an assistive device.

Calculators

Some children with special needs use calculators for specified types of math work. Obviously, calculator skills are taught to every elementary student. In the case of a child with a learning disability in math the calculator might be used more often.

Calculators are used when a student understands *how* to complete a math problem but gets overwhelmed with the calculations. Sometimes the child is not able to remember the basic math facts. Perhaps he understands that to get the average of a group of numbers he must add the numbers and then divide by how many numbers he added. Perhaps he understands the process but has difficulty remembering addition or division facts. He may be allowed to use a calculator if his IEP is so written. The same student would not be allowed to use a calculator for an assignment that practices or assesses knowledge of math facts because that would defeat the purpose of the assessment.

Writing Helps

Handheld electronic spell checkers are sometimes used by students with learning disabilities. The student can enter an attempted spelling and the device will give a list of correctly spelled word choices. At least some of these models will then "say" the word and its definition.

Spell checking devices are not only common for students with learning disabilities. They are widely used on computers and palm devices by many people without a disability.

Electronic Dictionaries

Electronic dictionaries are used by students with learning disabilities in later elementary grades and older. Like a spell checker, the dictionary will offer choices of words that are spelled correctly. An audio component of the dictionary will "speak" the word choices as well as their meanings, allowing the student to choose the word he needs.

Paper

Pressure-sensitive paper allows one or more copies to be made as someone writes. This kind of paper is often used for classroom note taking. A designated peer takes notes as the teacher talks. At the end of class, the top sheet is given to the student with special needs and the copy is kept by the note taker for her own use.

 Fact

The "best" student in the class may not be the wisest choice to be a note taker. Consider how thorough the student's notes are. Sometimes the top students do not see the need to take as many notes. Also consider the individual's handwriting skills; notes should be taken in clear, easy-to-read printing.

Paper with raised lines is sometimes used for students with vision impairments or with students having visual discrimination difficulties. The tactile feature of the paper allows the student to better judge where to write his letters and sentences.

Just for Fun

Gadgets are not limited to school help. By exercising care, you should be able to find games and toys at your local toy store to meet your child's needs and provide hours of fun. A shopping trip online to find specialized products can turn up many gizmos geared toward recreational fun.

Toys

Toys that light up (including balls and manipulative toys) can be fun for the child with low vision or the child who is autistic. Many light-up toys are sold in traditional toy stores, and a variety of companies that offer specialized toys can be found online.

Toys that make sounds are also favorites of children with low vision and those who are blind. Toys that vibrate are popular with children with various special needs (vision, hearing loss, and sensory integration).

Outdoor Fun

Some backyard fun items are traditional favorites, but offer added appeal to the child with special needs. Children with autism crave sensory input provided by trampolines and swings. Climbing toys offer a great way to work off energy for the child who is ADHD.

Messy tables are popular for imaginative play and sensory integration. A messy table is a great choice for outside play or in a floor-protected area inside. Children enjoy using small containers and handheld scoops to fill, dump, and refill. It is also fun to bury small toys and have a hunt to find them. The "messy" part can be water, sand, rice, and so forth, but should be chosen based on the safety needs of the child. All messy table fun should be closely supervised by an adult.

Some backyard toys are adapted to meet special needs. Adapted swings provide physical support. Velcro gloves and balls assist children with physical or coordination challenges in games of catch.

Sports Equipment

A variety of more serious adaptive sports equipment is available. Specialized skis, horseback riding equipment, baseball batting Ts, and beep baseballs are a few examples of adapted sports equipment.

Bowling ramps can be used for children and teens who have physical disabilities, particularly those who do not have the strength or muscle control to maneuver a bowling ball. The ramp is placed in front of the lane. Another person assists by placing the bowling ball at the top of the ramp. The bowler can push the ball (with little force), and it will begin rolling down the ramp and the bowling lane.

CHAPTER 14

Peers: Pressures and Positives

The word *peers* brings to mind good thoughts and some not-so-good situations. The influence of peers can be positive and motivating. A peer can encourage a teen to keep trying and then finally make the team. The influence of peers can also represent pressure to make poor choices, such as drinking, driving too fast, and other things that cause parents to lie awake at night. Peer influence is active in the life of every child and teen, regardless of disability.

Self-Concept

Young children are busy exploring the world around them. When they are two to three years old, they demonstrate parallel play. In other words, they play next to other children, but not necessarily with them. Around age three they begin to show more interest in playing with other children. This progression is also true for most children with special needs, although children with more severe cognitive delay are sometimes the exception. As children begin to be more aware of others, they begin to notice ways they are the same and ways they are not.

I Knew I Was Different

For some children with special needs, the awareness of being different comes a little later—as they begin to start traditional school in kindergarten. With a child receiving early childhood special education however, this awareness often comes with the give-and-take play of a child who is almost four.

Perhaps the child is playing with friends at the park. One child challenges the others to race to the slide. It is the first time that the little girl with the walker is keenly aware that she is different from her peers. Perhaps one boy calls to the others that his mom is handing out cookies. However, the little boy who is deaf is intent on making a road for his car. When he looks up a few minutes later, he realizes that his friends are not there.

 Essential

Plan playtime opportunities for your child to include others with similar special needs as well as with children who do not have a disability. Consider neighborhood friends and schoolmates to form play groups. Being comfortable with all of her peers will boost your child's self-esteem.

Strengths and Weaknesses

Strengths and weakness include more than just disabilities. There are things your child can do well because of her aptitude, and there are things she cannot do well—disability or not.

For example, a teen may have an aptitude for art. She is the person who designed the cover of the yearbook and made all the posters for the class president's campaign. The others do not think of her as disabled even though she goes to the special education resource room for reading and math. They just think of her as an amazing artist. She has an aptitude for art.

In the special education resource room another student hates art, and is doing well to draw a stick figure. In this scenario art aptitude has nothing to do with disability. You either can draw—or not.

Likes and Dislikes

Besides strengths and weaknesses, your child has her own set of likes and dislikes. Perhaps you have a teen and running cross-country comes easy for her because of her ADHD. She may like getting sweaty, but may not like putting in the extra hours to keep up with her schoolwork. Maybe you have a fourth-grade child who has a learning disability that results in difficulty remembering the words to songs, and yet she loves to sing.

Likes and dislikes are important for day-to-day satisfaction in hobbies. Sometimes people are fortunate enough to do something they really like for a living, but the best life success skill is self-awareness and acceptance. Enjoy exploring likes and dislikes with your teen. It is an important step in her being able to say "I like me!"

I Like Me

The bottom line on your child's interaction with peers is whether or not she has a positive self-concept. No one is good at everything, but by the same token, everyone has talents or aptitude in some area. Many children with Down syndrome are known for being very loving or kind. Some children with Asperger's syndrome have an incredible memory for detail.

Help your child on the journey of getting to know herself. Show her that you like the person she is. It is important that she be comfortable in her own skin.

Just Like the Others

Around ages ten or eleven it starts to hit hard. Kids just want to be like their peers. They want to look like them. Wanting to be like others is evident in social situations, at school, and even at home.

For example, children with hearing loss in the fourth grade become very reluctant to wear hearing aids because they do not want to look different. Leaving the inclusion classroom for special education becomes more upsetting to children with learning disabilities. They want to do the same things as their peers.

Siblings

Keep an eye out for sibling jealousy. Often we think of it from the perspective of the sibling who is "typically developing." She may see Mom and Dad's attention as more focused on helping her little brother with learning difficulties than being interested in her soccer tryouts. Most parents are quick to say that they love their children equally. The extraordinary need of one child, however, can come across very differently to a sibling who has a normally fragile self-concept.

 Fact

> Very few families experience a lack of sibling love and caring (even when the green-eyed monster is around). Draw on the bond that brothers and sisters continue to share. Encourage activities as a family as well as some just for siblings, to foster that healthy, supportive rapport.

Sibling jealousy can also go the other direction as well. Little brother who has learning difficulties can be frustrated with how easily his sister finishes her homework. On Friday evening, she is the one who is hanging out with friends. He wants to be invited to activities with the other children in his class. Seeing his sister go places with her friends, he may decide that certainly his parents are giving *her* more freedom or privileges.

Look for ways to point out how the strengths of siblings complement each other. Is one a great artist who makes the family proud by decorating birthday card envelopes? Is one more mechanically minded and able to fix that temperamental bike?

Kids at School

Your child may wish to be more like other kids at school. Perhaps he wishes he did not have to attend special education classes. Perhaps he longs to be more popular and confident.

Acknowledge how your child feels. His feelings are real; they impact his self-concept and how he approaches life. Real life, however, is not always fair.

 Essential

Work with your child's IEP team to plan which classes should be taken in the special education setting. Also look for opportunities to have your child in the inclusion class with his peers. He will take much of his cue from you on how to react to leaving his peers for specialized instruction.

Acknowledge how your child feels, and then talk about ideas to boost his self-confidence. Can he look for opportunities to answer questions in class? That will boost his self-concept and give him recognition in the eyes of his peers. Brainstorm about social situations. Can he invite a friend from his inclusion class to come over or to go to an activity like the movies? Acknowledge how your child feels, and then help him make a plan.

Others with Special Needs

Sometimes your child will feel jealousy toward another child with special needs. This may happen when he perceives the other child as being more successful. Perhaps he has the social language down pat, or his house is the cool place to be. Perhaps he is more successful in academics and does not have special education instruction for as many classes as your child does.

Help your child refocus on the great things about himself. What are his own achievements? Remind him that everyone has different goals. Perhaps he can pat himself on the back for practicing multi-plication facts daily until he mastered them.

Social Behaviors

Some children need more feedback on social behaviors. This is often the case for tweens. A tween with Down syndrome might almost be old enough to be considered a teenager, and yet may have the cognitive understanding of a preschooler. In society—at school, in the mall, in restaurants, everywhere your child goes—she is first judged by her size.

Social Behavior at Home

Encourage your child to practice appropriate social behavior at home. Let her give you a goodnight kiss, but if you have friends over for dinner, remind her that it is good manners to *say* goodnight. Expect that she will be fully dressed when she is at home.

Your child may see things from a young point of view, but she will understand and follow your expectations for social behavior.

Time with Friends

Social behavior with friends should be very well-defined. Your child will be much more successful at following your guidelines if she knows what they are!

You can define time expectations for a teen with a learning disability by purchasing a watch for her. Teach her how to set the alarm. Then have her set the time you will meet her in the mall. She can shop with a friend without losing track of the time, and meet you when you agreed, to ask for money for the big sale!

Social Words

Social words are as important as social behaviors. Your child's choice of words will often determine how another person will react to him. Remember that you are your child's coach in social conversations. Although he may see a speech and language therapist, you will be with him in a wide variety of social situations outside of school.

Manners

Social words show manners (or a lack of them). *Please* and *thank you* are obviously in good taste. Talk with your child about polite things to say and when to stop a conversation.

Your child may be very interested in asking people their ages. Remind him that this is okay if he is talking to children or teens. Otherwise, it is considered poor manners.

 Fact

> Understanding the meaning behind words may be difficult for your child. Many children with special needs take expressions literally. If you say that it is raining cats and dogs, for example, your child may do a double-take. He may know that animals are not falling from the sky, but he may not understand the true meaning of the idiom.

Give your child feedback and guidance on his choice of words. A child with a cognitive delay may think nothing of telling a house guest that he loves them. That would likely be an inappropriate comment if the child is nearing his teens unless, of course, the visitors are his grandparents. Talk about the words that are socially acceptable. In this case, suggest "I am happy you came to visit" or "It is nice to see you again."

You cannot prepare your child for every type of social conversation. Explain that if you or the other person gets a puzzled or alarmed look, then it is time to stop. He may not be using good manners.

Asking for Help

Your child may have difficulty asking questions. Whether he is asking for help or asking for specific information, he may have trouble putting his thoughts into words.

Many children on the autism spectrum are impulsive. If a child sees his favorite kind of cookie in someone else's lunch, he may simply take it. The impulse was greater than his sense of social awareness and his ability to ask for a cookie.

Give your child lots of practice asking questions. Expect him to ask (and ask politely) when he wants a snack or when he needs help tying his shoes. If he has trouble getting started, prompt him with the beginning of the question: *Start with:* "May I . . ."

Here are some common question words:

- Who
- What
- Where
- When
- Why
- Will

- Can
- Do/does
- Was/were
- Are/is
- How much/many/ often/far

All children learn *Who* and *What* first. *Why* tends to be easy to ask, but it is the most difficult to answer.

Conversations with Peers

Your child's speech and language therapist or your other children can be helpful by practicing peer conversations. They will be able to explain the lingo used by their peers. They will also be able to help your child understand words to watch out for because they may have a distasteful social meaning. Your child doesn't need to know all the details of each word's meaning, but he will be more prepared when encountering these words if he knows they are not polite.

Teasing

Children tease each other. Often there is no cruel or hidden intent, just a thoughtless word or deed. Children with special needs can ward off many thoughtless situations with a few simple guidelines.

Hurtful Words

Whether or not the speaker's intent was to hurt, he will likely continue if he sees that your child reacts by being upset. Talk with your child about ignoring hurtful words. Talk with her about making eye contact with the speaker, but not showing upset.

Then explain that, sadly, some people continue to say hurtful things. It is wise to just ignore those people and seek out other playmates.

Hurtful Actions

Everyone wants to be included. Hurtful actions can mean not being included in play or conversation. It might mean not being chosen for a team or not being invited to a get-together.

Make sure your child knows you understand that she feels hurt by being excluded from an activity. Explain that sometimes there is a reason that was not meant to be hurtful. Perhaps the other child did not realize that your daughter wanted to play, or was allowed to invite only four friends to sleep over.

Perhaps the other child did make an intentional poor choice. Help your child move on by planning something that is special to her.

Physical Hurts

Assure your child that physical hurting is never okay. If she is physically hurt, she should remain calm and report the physical hurt to an adult.

Talking to a teacher or staff member about a physical hurt at school can be tough. Your child may be afraid that teasing will follow. Explain that it is not okay for anyone to hurt another person. If necessary, go with your child to talk to the appropriate adult.

You can reinforce this concept at home by repeating it when a sibling may resort to hitting. That will help your child vocalize her concerns at school.

Social Invitations

Social invitations can be as simple as an offer to play jump rope or as complicated as going to the prom. Most children and teens with special needs are as concerned about social invitations as their peers. Some children on the autism spectrum, some children with low cognitive abilities, and some with behavior disorders are not as aware or concerned.

Sibling Invitations

Often social invitations come from a child's siblings and the siblings' friends. Being included for a movie or a trip to the mall can be a very positive experience. Encourage your children to include each other in activities, and to do things with their own groups of friends to avoid resentments.

Peers with Special Needs

Your child will have friends from his special education program. Because these programs often draw from a larger area than the neighborhood school, it will be a little harder for you to organize time for your child to see his friends.

If your child's friends will need a parent to accompany them, consider the following regular get-togethers:

- A regular afternoon at the park
- After-school pizza and a movie
- A mini bowling league
- Swim time

Look again at your schedule and prioritize get-togethers for your child and his friends. You don't have to drop everything or only focus on making this happen, but realize that a consistent effort will have a big payoff for your child's self esteem.

Peers Without Special Needs

If your child is in an inclusion classroom for part of the day, he will have friends without special needs. For some children with learning disabilities, this is a natural occurrence. Having difficulty with reading has nothing to do with success at baseball. Not remembering math facts does not impact clothes fashion.

Encouraging "friend time" with these peers is also important. As an adult, your child will function in a world where there is no separation between those with special needs and those without. It is critical for him to be involved and feel comfortable with all of his peers.

Making your child's socialization a priority is again necessary (but should not be all-encompassing). There may be some awkwardness or social ice to be broken because your child leaves the "regular" classroom for special education services, but socialization and appropriate education are equally important for the development of your child.

Dating

As they approach their tween and teen years, children become more aware of the opposite sex and want to spend more time together. Set your ground rules and make sure your expectations are clear.

See if your community has a location for teens with special needs to get together. If nothing is available, consider recruiting other parents to organize something on a regular basis. Music, dancing, movies, pizza, and bowling are popular with most crowds. The key is to make this a time with supervision but minimal parent involvement.

Parties

Children and teens love parties. They represent a special kind of social invitation as well as celebration. Many times, a child with special needs feels left out of the party scene.

Birthday Parties

Families usually have a limited amount of space for young party-goers. So, either a birthday party will include the whole class and be held outside the home, or only a few will be invited.

Sometimes being on the inviting side of the table is the first step to being included. Consider if your child will invite a few close friends or have a large party that includes everybody in the class. If your child's school allows birthday treats, this can be a solution. Then it's easier to invite only a few close friends to a home party.

Boy-Girl Parties

As your child reaches the age for boy-girl parties, be very specific about your expectations. Keep in mind that impulsivity in a child with ADHD, autism, or a behavior concern plays a role in every life situation. Find out about a party your child will be attending. Where will it be? Who will be supervising? Who will be going?

Smoking and Drugs

Your child's school will probably initiate discussions about smoking and drugs. Use the materials your child brings home as the springboard for your family discussions.

Reread the smoking and drug information with your tween and talk about the vocabulary and ideas. Explain to your tween that she will be in situations when she has to make a choice. Because you will not be with her wherever she goes, it is important to talk with her ahead of time.

Peer Pressures

Your child will not be exempt from peer pressures. Impulsivity and lack of education are two factors that can give peer pressure the upper hand. Help your tween prepare for peer pressures by making sure she is aware of the dangers and the consequences.

 Fact

You and your spouse are the most influential role models for your tween. What you say does not matter nearly as much as what you do. If you are saying "Don't smoke" but you smoke, your tween will hear your actions loud and clear.

Communication

Keep the lines of communication open on all topics. Talking about smoking and drugs once would be like telling a young child just one time to look both ways before crossing the street. If you never tell the child again, will she be likely to remember? Talk often (don't preach) with your teen. Remember, too, that the lines of communication go both ways. Listen to your tween and to her friends. Listen.

Sex Education

Sex education will also be covered in school. A unit in school, however, is not enough to communicate your family's values.

Teens (regardless of cognitive ability) go through all the stages of physical development and desire. Talk with your tween about these changes before they happen. Communicating an understanding of sexual issues is an opportunity to use all of the skills you have practiced throughout your child's life: clear, concrete explanation; discussion of social situations and language; reminder of expectations; appropriate supervision; and lots of listening.

CHAPTER 15

Extracurricular Activities

Extracurricular activities are important in preparation for real life. No doubt your child will meet a number of people with different backgrounds and experiences through extracurricular activities. Some will be helpful, and others will need guidance about how to interact with a child with special needs. There will be times when your child must communicate information about his disability. He will gain experience being his own advocate. He will also have the opportunity to try new things, to build his social skills and confidence, and above all—to have fun!

Assess Abilities and Needs

Some extracurricular activities are purely for fun. Others require a certain level of ability. Making a good match between the activity and your child's unique abilities, interests, and needs is the first step.

Talent

What are your child's talents? Is she a strong athlete? Does she rally her peers to support a cause? Does she organize a campsite with little difficulty before exploring the outdoors?

Help your child consider her talents when choosing an activity for her free time. In some instances, you may see an aptitude or talent that your child has not yet recognized. Encourage, but don't force, her to explore those areas.

Special Needs

Talk with your child about her unique needs. Disability does not mean lack of ability. It does mean that she may need support to be successful with her chosen activity. In some instances a disability presents a safety concern. Work with your child to find activities that promote her personal development without putting her in physical danger.

 Essential

> Your child should be able to explain her disability by the time she completes grade school. She should know how it impacts her unique needs at school, at home, and in the community. Remind your child that her unique needs do not cancel her responsibilities, only the way in which they are accomplished.

Enjoyment Factor

Extracurricular activities should be challenging. They should provide relaxation, satisfaction, and in most cases—socialization. Above all, they should be enjoyable.

Talk to your child about the kinds of things she likes to do. Here are some questions to get you started:

- What is your favorite thing to do outdoors?
- What do you like best about rainy days?
- Would you rather do something just by yourself or with some friends?
- Is doing art projects at school fun?
- Tell me something that would be fun to learn.

Consider Interests

Your child may have ability in areas that are not of high interest to him. Extracurricular activities are pastimes and should be enjoyable. They are not schoolwork or jobs. Talk with your child about his interests. For example:

- Athletics: Athletics is an area where many children with special needs excel; their learning disability may only impact schoolwork. In many cases, the athletic ability of the child will shine given the opportunity.
- Art and Music: Is your child interested in the arts? Music is an area of enjoyment for many children. In fact, music is used to teach everything from math facts to the names of the states and capitals. Music seems to go beyond barriers.
- Community Service: Some children and teens are drawn to community service; they want to be involved in helping others. School clubs and community groups organize activities that range from food drives to picking up litter in the park.

Choose Activities

Our society offers lots of choices for free time. Your child will not be able to sign up for everything, so you'll need to help her select. Sometimes it is helpful to offer your child options rather than asking her to express her interests. Ask if she would like to try activity A or activity B instead of what activity she would like to try this fall. Children who are autistic, in particular, do better with choices than open-ended questions. Beyond interests and special needs you will need to consider some other factors when choosing extracurricular activities.

Age Considerations

A young child needs some unplanned time to explore the world around her. As that child gets older, she may be ready to participate in some group activities. Many parents see activities as a means to establishing a schedule. Schedules are helpful for children with learning disabilities or autism and those with cognitive delays. Every moment, however, should not be scheduled, much less filled with activities. Young children need some time to figure out what to do next. It is an important part of developing problem-solving skills and creativity. Teens also need opportunities to pursue personal interests and hobbies and to learn to pitch in as a family member.

Realistic Commitments

How many activities can your child really stay involved and be interested in? Mental focus can be stretched too far. Children with learning disabilities especially need to focus on a reasonable amount of activity. Too many parts to the schedule or too many new situations (and rules) can be overwhelming for them.

Balance with Schoolwork

Even with modifications and accommodations, schoolwork will likely take your child longer to complete than it does for her siblings. Re-explanation and supervision of your child's homework will likely take a large amount of your own time as well.

Take schoolwork into consideration when signing up for extracurricular activities. Perhaps a good plan is to be more involved in activities in the summer when there is no homework.

Choose a Group

Another part of the extracurricular decision involves the kind of group your child will choose. You and your child may have a strong preference based on where his friends are or because of specific communication needs. Or you may prefer that he has the opportunity to branch out to have new experiences and meet new people.

School Groups

Schools typically offer a number of clubs and organizations. These offerings increase as your child goes into middle school and high school. The faculty advisors of school clubs will have some experience with students with special needs from their teaching. The special educators in the school can also provide information about how to meet the needs of your child for extracurricular activities.

 Essential

Let the school bus company, as well as the school, know when your child will not be riding the bus home. Remind your child who will be picking him up after the activity is finished. Having him write a note to himself in his assignment notebook is a good way to eliminate confusion.

Another advantage of a school group is that meetings are often right after school. Transportation to the activity is not a problem, but transportation home may have to be specially scheduled. If your child normally rides the bus home, he will need alternate transportation after a club meeting.

Another advantage to a school group is the opportunity to socialize with peers from a number of classes. Friendships often form as a result of club involvement. There is also an increased sense of school pride.

Community Groups

Some activities are not offered through schools. If your child is interested in learning how to train the family dog, for example, he will need to look for a community group that focuses on animal care.

Involvement in a community group broadens your child's social contacts and builds self-esteem. Some community groups offer programs for people of all ages. If your child becomes involved with a community group, it may be an activity that he can continue as an adult.

Groups with Special Needs

If your child has more complicated special needs, you may decide to choose a group especially for children with disabilities. For example, if a child in a wheelchair wants to bowl, he may sign up for a bowling league that will use ramps and have volunteers to assist the bowlers. A child who is blind might enjoy outings with a group from a vision program. It would be much more fun to go to the zoo with this group and pet the animals in the children's zoo, than to "see" the animals from afar in the main part of the zoo.

Family Activity Schedule

There is only so much time in the day and there is only so much money in the checking account. The car can only go so many places. Your child is part of a family, so consider the big picture when deciding on activities for each child.

Plan the overall commitment to activities so that everyone is treated fairly. That does not mean that everyone has to have the same number of activities; age and stamina of each child should be considered. Include activities for Mom and Dad as well.

Talk with your children about the activities of your family. Discuss whether a child will be allowed to participate in another activity after school is out for the summer. If one child is making a big time commitment to a sport, talk about what her homework schedule will look like. The more children understand why things are arranged as they are, the smoother the schedule will go.

Fact

Children with special needs work very hard at school. They work to improve academic skills and often attend therapy. When they go home, they still have homework to complete. Evaluate your child's stamina at the end of the day. Does she have the time and energy to go to an extracurricular activity? Make careful choices about extracurricular activities.

Arrange transportation with other families to save on time and gas. Talk with the other parents about your child's unique medical and communication needs. Provide them with your contact information in case of an emergency.

Check to make sure that family down time is a regular part of the schedule. Sometimes your family needs to have nothing to do—as a group. If an activity is always planned, your children will not know how to interact with each other without this focus.

Sports

Sports seem like a natural extracurricular activity and in most communities, sport teams are available to children starting at a very young age. However, playing on a team may not be the best choice for your child.

Ability

While your child does not have to be a pro to play sports, he will feel more comfortable if he has a certain level of ability. Large-muscle coordination, hand-eye coordination, and the ability to run should be considered. A child may want to participate in a sport despite challenges, while other children do not find it at all fun. Look for other activities that will be fun for them.

Practice

Being a part of a sports team requires practice (with the team as well as individually), but many children do not understand the practice behind the game. Talk to your child about the time and effort commitment before signing up. How will practice impact other activities and schoolwork?

Sportsmanship

Playing on a team requires sportsmanship. While this can be character-building, it can also be frustrating for the impulsive or easily angered child.

Does your child take medication during the school day? Does he take it outside of school time? Talk to your child's coach about medical considerations that will impact how your child gets along with others and follows directions.

Team Support

Sometimes playing sports may not be the best choice of activity for a child. It may not be a good physical or emotional match, and yet the child may still be very interested in being on the team.

Many community teams and school teams are open to someone helping the team in other ways. Being a team manager, helping with equipment, or otherwise assisting the team may be an option.

Clubs

Clubs offer fun and challenging activities as well as a sense of belonging. In addition to the clubs offered by schools, a wide variety of clubs are offered in communities. Consider volunteering in a club that interests your child. You'll be offering him support as well as building awareness of ways to include children with special needs.

Scouting

Boys and girls enjoy and learn from scouting. Because of these organizations' teamwork approach, they are great options for many kids with special needs. Scout activities provide a blend of hands-on practice and book learning. Everyone wants those badges, so the motivation to read is heightened.

Skills Clubs

Skills clubs offer a good fit for children who have a very specific interest, such as horsemanship, martial arts, or homemaking skills. Like scouting, skills clubs offer hands-on activities and book study components. Skills clubs also include competition, which appeals to many kids with behavioral concerns.

Just-for-Fun Classes

Just-for-fun classes are similar to skills clubs. They focus on a particular area of interest, and are conducted by a teacher with expertise in that area. Children from a wide variety of backgrounds and academic ability attend these classes.

Hobbies

Art and music classes teach children hobbies. Learning to play a guitar is not only an enjoyable pastime, it offers your child another way to interact with his peers. Art is too often left out of the school curriculum. Developing an artistic ability also can lead to a lifelong hobby and even a future career.

If your child does not attend a hobby class, help him explore other hobby ideas. Creating a collection, biking, playing board games, baking, reading, and crafts are great hobbies. Planning a time to participate in the hobby with your child is a way to maintain a strong parent-child bond.

Exercise

Exercise classes come in many forms. Some are simply exercise for its own sake. Others incorporate martial arts skills or dance. Consider a type of exercise class to help your child with coordination, stress relief, and self-confidence.

Learning

Learning a foreign language or how to build a model rocket are just two examples of just-for-fun classes. School basics of reading, writing, and arithmetic can't cover everything. Talk to your child about what he wants to learn, and then check community centers and libraries for just-for-fun learning classes.

Planned Gatherings

Some children just want to be with their friends in their free time, and some kids (those with more severe cognitive delays or involved physical impairments, for example) may not be well-suited for typical extracurricular activities. Consider creating an extracurricular activity that will meet the needs of your child.

Form a Social Group

Contact other families to establish a group. Have a basic plan in mind, but brainstorm with other parents as well.

When setting up the planning meeting pick an evening or weekend time so more people can attend. Even though you will meet to plan activities for your children, ask that the kids stay home during this planning time.

Set the Schedule

Establishing a schedule is a solid step in getting your social group off the ground. If families know that the social group will be every Saturday afternoon, they can plan their schedules accordingly.

Choose a Location

Where the social groups will meet largely depends on the group's activity and the physical needs of the participants. Suppose that you are planning a movie night and most of the attendees use wheelchairs. Having the movie night in someone's home is not practical. Instead, contact a community center, church, or school to see if you can use a room for the event.

As much as possible, have the event in the same location every time. With a designated place and time, you will eliminate the risk of someone not knowing where to go or showing up on the wrong day.

Occasionally, you may want the social group to go on outings. Make flyers well in advance of the outing so that every family has the needed information. An e-mail reminder the day before is also a good idea.

When setting up your group, consider how your child and his friends will be able to voice their opinions. Will they be able to vote on the next movie? Will they be able to select the refreshments from several choices? Allowing them to be a part of the planning empowers them to be more independent.

Who Will Do What

You may be the organizing force behind your child's social group, but for the group to really take off and remain stable, you will need others to help you. Take time at the organizational meeting to divide up the work. You will likely need the following:

- Refreshment coordinator
- Entertainment coordinator
- Special events and outings planner
- Publicity coordinator

At first, your social group may not be large enough to need one person (or a group) for each job. Doubling up on the work until the group grows is a good way to get the ball rolling.

CHAPTER 16

Travel Tips

People travel for a variety of reasons: business, family obligations, medical appointments, pleasure, and special events. The type and extent of travel that is good for your child depends on her unique needs. A child with a severe physical disability and extensive medical needs might seldom travel—except to medical appointments and possibly to visit close relatives. Packing the needed equipment might be impossible because of its size, volume, and sensitivity. Most children can travel, though, and a trip will be enjoyable for all with careful and thorough planning in advance.

Destinations

Lots of families travel to family functions, and for fun. Trips that fit your budget may not be as frequent and the destinations may not be as far as in the past, but travel planning will still demand your attention. Travel for the child with a special need without any preparation will be far from fun and games, but with a little planning you can find the best choices for your family's time away from home.

Day Trips

Some kids enjoy taking a day trip more than travel to stay overnight. The advantages of a day trip include:

- Lower cost
- Returning to the comforts of home at night
- Packing supplies for one day (no PJs, etc. needed)
- Does not require extended time off of work
- Ability to choose departure and return home time

Families who live close to a large city will have lots of day-trip options. Those who live in more rural areas will not have as many destinations (museums, zoo, theme parks), but can make up for it with outdoor activities (swimming, fishing, picnics).

When considering a day trip, planning the destination is important. Consider times that your child will be at his best. A tired child (with or without a disability) will not enjoy the outing. Also consider when the destination will be least crowded. If you go to the science museum during the school week, you will likely encounter large school groups. Going on a sunny Sunday afternoon in the summer might avoid the crowds (as others are outside) and be a pleasant escape from the heat.

If you are going to a business or tourist-type attraction, research the hours, admission fees, and any information about services for children with disabilities. If your child is deaf, for example, find out the times that presentations are interpreted in sign language.

Perhaps you are planning a day in the great outdoors. Plan for the necessities: bathrooms, snacks, drinks, and a place to come in from the elements. Remember sunscreen, bug spray, and routine medications as well as emergency contact numbers.

Visits to Family and Friends

You may want, or need, to travel to see family and friends. This can be one of the most relaxing travel destinations, or it can be one of the most stressful.

Begin by planning ahead with the host family. While they do not need to know all of your child's confidential information, some basic explanation of what to expect can make the visit much smoother. Consider sharing information on the following:

- Dietary needs
- Mode of communication
- Sensitivity to touch, light, sound
- Interaction with strangers
- Favorite pastimes

If Aunt Susie always grabs and hugs her young visitors, a heads-up can prevent a child on the autism spectrum from having an unpleasant encounter. If Cousin Mike likes to take the kids to the park, make sure he is aware if your child has a unilateral hearing loss. It will prevent frustration for them both and possible danger to your child as they are crossing the street.

Perhaps you will be visiting someone who adores children and will definitely go out of her way to interact with your child. Suggest a preferred activity or favorite snack to set the tone for the visit. Once your hostess sees that some tried and true ideas are the ways to make friends, she will be asking for more input.

Vacations

Choose a vacation destination that suits the overall needs of your family. There should be something for everyone—things that will appeal to your child, his siblings, you, and your spouse. If the destination only offers activities that differ greatly from your child's needs, perhaps it is a trip for siblings to take with one or both parents at a different time.

Theme parks offer a variety of activities: shows, rides, visits with movie or cartoon characters, and playgrounds. If your child has a physical disability, you will be able to bypass long lines for rides, but the same is not true for other disabilities. The child with ADHD may love the thrill of the roller coasters, but he may grow impatient as he waits for his turn to ride. Theme parks also require lots of walking.

Scenic areas can offer a calming get-away-from-it-all option. Some children on the autism spectrum respond well to this kind of a trip. Camping can offer the same peaceful experience for some. However, the child with ADHD or the child who is overly sensitive to sun and bugs may not enjoy such a trip.

Whatever your vacation destination, consider your accommodations, food choices, and the activities that will entertain your family. Doing research ahead of time will help you effectively plan the trip, avoiding things that will cause upset to your child and to your family.

Special Events

Sometimes families must travel for special events. You can pick and choose some of the special travel for your family, but some of it will be unavoidable. Plan ahead to avoid easily prevented frustrations.

Weddings and Funerals

No humor intended, weddings and funerals have some similarities for the child with special needs:

- These events are short, very intense encounters with lots of people. You should look for a place of quiet regrouping away from the crowds.
- They can disrupt your child's eating routine. Come armed with simple snacks (to be eaten at an appropriate time).
- They might be difficult for your child to understand. Bring some quiet activities (books, crayons and paper, calming music on an iPod, a stress ball).
- They require special, uncomfortable clothing. Choose something appropriate for your child to wear, but pick your

battles. It won't be the end of the world if he wears a nice but comfortable shirt instead of a collar and tie.

- They require certain social behaviors: quiet talking or no talking, at least basic response during conversations, and patient waiting. Talk with your child ahead of time about expected behavior.

Of course, there are some differences between weddings and funerals. You should have a plan for a wedding reception. If you and your spouse plan to stay for a long reception, you may wish to make arrangements for child care.

The funeral of a family member calls for extra care and attention. If your child is mature enough to visit the funeral home, plan to go at a time when there will be fewer people. For the funeral, sit in a place that will allow an inconspicuous exit if needed.

Holiday Travel

Many children with special needs, particularly those on the autism spectrum or with behavior disorders, thrive on routine. These children depend on routine to help them predict what will happen. Without it, they may be overwhelmed by not knowing how to react in new situations. You can ease the change in routine that comes with holiday travel by doing the following:

- Preparing your child by talking about the *who, what, where,* and *when* of the visit. Mark her activity calendar and use family pictures to make it visual.
- Creating a visit routine that includes a sleep schedule and a balance of fun activities and quiet time.
- Taking along some comforts of home. Snacks and favorite toys can help your child deal with so many unfamiliar things happening around her.
- Talking to Grandma ahead of time. Explain the kind of routines that work so that she is not offended when your child

really needs a nap, but Grandma wants to visit Santa for pictures at a crowded mall.

- Cutting yourself some slack. A busy holiday visit will bring some unexpected happenings and not all will be pleasant. Look for the positives and enjoy the visit.

To a lesser degree, children with hearing loss and those with ADHD are also dependent on routine. Special activities and travel at the holidays can be frustrating and overwhelming for these kids and consequently for their families.

When planning holiday travel, be aware that your child may easily get to the "on overload" point. It seems like a trip to Grandma's out of state with five cousins will be fun. Take extra measures to increase the chances of that fun happening.

Family Reunions

Travel to a family reunion can be a great way to see lots of relatives at once, but the sheer numbers can be overwhelming for your child. Following the guidelines for holiday travel can help. There are two additional keys to family reunion visits.

 Essential

Use family photos to talk to your child about an upcoming visit with family or friends. The photos can include people and the places you will visit. Remembering the fish aquarium at Uncle Joe's or the slide in Cousin Jake's backyard can help your child look for the familiar upon arrival, instead of feeling overwhelmed that everything is new.

First, make sure that you have your child's comfort foods in tow. Even if she does not have special dietary needs, she may not be prepared for Aunt Sally's spicy pasta salad and Cousin Lizzie's pickled beets. Remember that the foods you loved while growing up will most likely be foreign to your child. Having some familiar favorites will help her smile as her cheeks are pinched and she hears yet again how much she has grown.

Second, plan for a quiet place for your child to rest and pull herself together. It does not matter if she is five or fifteen, having a place to get away from the reunion hubbub will make it more enjoyable for everyone. The quiet place might be a room away from the family action, a nearby relative's home, or even a quiet hotel room.

Transportation

Once you have decided on a travel destination, you need to consider how to travel. The decision to travel by car, plane, bus, or train will depend in part on your child's needs. In most cases, there is no one single transportation choice that is best—each mode has its benefits and drawbacks.

Travel by Car

Making a trip by car is often the first choice of families with a child with special needs. A car (van, SUV) gives parents the most control over travel details that will impact their child, such as:

- Departure time
- Frequency and timing of stops
- Availability of transportation throughout the trip
- Ability to take more things
- Familiarity of the vehicle
- Use of DVD players and radio
- Ability to talk without disturbing other travelers

Air Travel

Some families find air travel a good match for their needs, particularly when time is an issue or when traveling long distances.

A parent traveling alone with one or more children also has some support from airline personnel.

 Alert

Early boarding is available from every airline if your child requires additional time or help. Plan to arrive early enough to sit in the preboarding area near the gate. When early boarding is announced, you will have the least distance to go and your child will not be overwhelmed and frustrated with the group of waiting passengers.

Travel by plane, however, does have some drawbacks. An airplane is obviously a small, contained area. In general, passengers are quiet and stay in their seats. This can be frustrating for a child who needs to move around. You can avoid some of his discomfort by planning additional physical activity before boarding the plane. Give him the opportunity to walk to the boarding gate or at least around the waiting area.

Allowing your child to help carry a small bag or backpack can provide the "weight bearing" needed to tire him out and to help him sit quietly on the plane. Note that the bag he carries should be moderately heavy *for him*. The goal is not to have him carry the family luggage for the trip.

Travel by Bus

Travel by bus can be a cost-efficient mode of transportation, but it is often more restricting than air travel. With high-back seating and a single aisle to the bathroom (if there is one), some children feel too boxed in. Buses do make scheduled rest stops, but not stops for the travelers' requests. The parent(s) traveling with a child with special needs will have little or no assistance getting him on and off of the bus.

Travel by Train

Travel by train has been a popular and necessary choice in Europe for many years. Its use in the United States has varied throughout our country's history. It seems to be on the rise now with the escalating cost of gasoline.

Travel by train offers a mass transportation option with lower fees than airfare and more conveniences than bus travel. Train conductors assist passengers with physical needs and parents with young children as they board and exit the train.

Although other passengers are in the same car, there is more room to move about. Some seats are arranged so that four people may face each other, with a table in the center. This offers a convenient means of having snacks and engaging in other activities (games, coloring, simple puzzles) to pass the time.

Lodging

Unless you are taking a day trip, you will need to consider lodging accommodations for your family. Some children love hotels with swimming pools and those magical vending machines. Others are overwhelmed with unfamiliar surroundings.

The Home of Family or Friends

Perhaps you will be visiting the home of family or friends. In some instances, this can be reassuring to the child with special needs. For example, an autistic child thrives on routine and predictable environments. Grandma's house might provide that—unless she rearranges her furniture often. Even a simple change like new dishes could be upsetting to the child who is counting on things to be the same.

Talk to your hostess ahead of time. Try to give her a glimpse of how your child functions at home. See "Visits to Family and Friends" at the beginning of this chapter.

Hotels

Sometimes hotels are an alternative to staying at the too busy/too noisy/too crowded home of a friend or relative. A hotel room can offer a place for your family to have some privacy and to regroup. Hotel swimming pools are a great place for many kids with special needs to relax. Water is therapeutic for many, and it offers included-in-the-price family fun.

 Essential

Remember that a child on the autism spectrum recognizes the smallest differences in routine and physical setting. If she is dependent on routine and a predictable environment, staying overnight away from home can be disturbing. She may spend the entire time getting used to her new surroundings.

Hotels do have some drawbacks. Unless your family has stayed at the same motel previously (*and* it has not changed its décor *and* you have the same room), the environment will be different to your child.

RVs and Tents

Some families avoid the upsetting lodging dilemma by taking home with them. Using an RV or even camping in a tent allows them to keep the setting relatively the same. The family has its privacy and does not have to be concerned with others in close proximity. If public restrooms and showers are used, however, that can upset an otherwise peaceful arrangement.

Timeshares

Another home-away-from-home option is staying at a timeshare type of property. Timeshare property might be something in which you have partial ownership, a place that you are renting from the owners, or a property owned and used by your extended family.

Like Grandma's house, it is a familiar environment as long as things have not been replaced or rearranged. If furniture has been moved, you may find yourself putting things back so that you and your child can rest easy!

If you are aware ahead of time that changes have been made, you can prepare your child by showing her pictures (the before-and-after kind of snapshots) before you arrive. When she sees the new arrangement, she may still be upset, but at least she won't be surprised by the differences.

Packing Checklist

Develop a master packing list that you can use for all of your trips. From necessity, you are probably a master at being prepared for any situation or emergency, but everyone needs a checklist when they are packing in the midst of the busyness of every day.

Clothes

Pack a variety and pack extra. You needn't pack every article of clothing that your child owns, especially if you will have access to a washer and dryer, but you should, however, be prepared for temperature changes. Layers of clothing work well during the seasons when temperatures are unpredictable.

CLOTHING PACKING LIST
- ✓ Pants
- ✓ Shirts
- ✓ Underwear
- ✓ Socks
- ✓ Shoes
- ✓ Pajamas
- ✓ Jacket or sweater

✓ Umbrella
✓ Blanket and pillow
✓ Coat, hat, gloves, and boots (for cold weather)
✓ Bibs (for infants or children with exceptional feeding needs)

You should also be prepared for spills and accidents. Even if you travel light and Grandma's washer is waiting to be used, you will want to include clothing changes.

Entertainment

You may be looking forward to catching up on old times with your college roommate, or you might be looking forward to sleeping in and enjoying some of Mom's great home cooking. Although your child might share your excitement for the trip, he will need some activities to pass the time or at least fill in the gaps.

ENTERTAINMENT PACKING LIST
✓ Small manipulative toys
✓ Books for independent reading and for reading with a parent
✓ Crayons and coloring books or paper
✓ Paper and pencil for older children
✓ Sports equipment
✓ DVDs, CDs, video and conventional games, music

Plan which activities you can take that will offer entertainment that's not disruptive. That is not to say that you should park your child in front of a television set for the duration of your visit. However, if he lives to watch a popular cartoon, pack those DVDs to take along for breaks. Your child deserves to relax on the trip as much as you do.

Not every child is "hooked" on DVDs. Some are obsessed with other kinds of technology. Some child love more traditional activities (books, sports, art, cars, or dolls). The idea is to pack some familiar kinds of activities that will pass the time.

Medical Supplies and Special Equipment

Consider whether or not your child will need medical supplies or specialized equipment on the trip. It may seem like this is obvious to include on your packing list, but a complete checklist can prevent scrambling to find a needed item in an unfamiliar area.

MEDICAL SUPPLIES AND SPECIAL EQUIPMENT PACKING LIST

✓ Orthopedic equipment
✓ Feeding equipment
✓ Oxygen (if needed)
✓ Medications: _____
✓ Emergency contact information: doctors, pharmacies, relatives
✓ Emergency information for the destination: hospitals and pharmacies
✓ General medical supplies: sunscreen, lotion for sunburn, vitamins, antiseptic, bandages, pain relievers, thermometer
✓ Other needed items: _____

As you travel, make revisions to your packing lists. When preparing for future trips, you will be able to tell quickly whether or not you remembered everything.

Travel Variations

Every trip will not be right for every family member. Sometimes it may be necessary for only several members of the family to travel for a specific purpose. At other times, it will be appropriate to take the whole family.

The Family

If your family is traveling to visit relatives or family friends, you may opt to travel with the whole family. You may also consider traveling together for the annual family vacation or a long get-away weekend. There are times, though, when only part of the family will go. Perhaps you're traveling for a particular event, such as a cousin's graduation, and the seating is limited. Perhaps it is an event that interests only part of the family, such as a truck show or a music festival.

Sometimes the decision to travel with only part of the family will be based on a child's special needs and the needs of the siblings and parents. That is not to say that the child should be excluded from family travel, but she may enjoy and be able to participate in certain travel activities more than others. She and her siblings may have their own travel experiences.

Travel with Part of the Family

A child and one or both of her parents may travel separately because of a special interest, ability, or the need to have one-on-one time. A child with limited cognitive ability might enjoy attending a musical performance with costume characters that would not appeal to her teenage siblings. Likewise, they may be interested in exploring a science museum that would not be of interest to their sister.

Consider a balance of whole-family travel and separate activities. The key is to include activities, travel, and outings that everyone can enjoy together or separately. See Chapter 8 for more ideas. Likewise, Mom and Dad need their own travel time. This is compounded in the situation of a single-parent home (see Chapter 5).

CHAPTER 17

Life Skills

E very parent thinks about her child's life as an adult. A long-range plan and well-developed life skills are needed. Consider the areas discussed in this chapter as you assist your child in developing the skill set to get along in day-to-day living. You may find that siblings or other family members need to step in to help the adult with special needs. The goal is, of course, to equip your child through planning, resources, learning, strategies, and a network of support to live successfully—and possibly independently.

Basic Self-Care

One of the most basic of living skills is personal self-care. Self-care is a priority regardless of living arrangement: family home, group home, or independent apartment. Teach basic self-care at the youngest age possible. Increase your expectations as your child grows in skill and maturity.

Hygiene

Teach hand washing before meals, after using the bathroom, before and after preparing food, after using cleaners or other chemicals (such as car oil, gas, pesticides, paints), and any time the hands are just plain dirty. If this habit begins when your child is very young, it will continue consistently throughout adulthood.

A bathing and shampooing routine should also be taught. If needed, make a chart for your child to check off each hygiene task as it is done. Young girls should also be taught about feminine hygiene as they approach the tween years.

Dental

Dental care began even before your child's birth as his teeth formed from his mother's calcium-rich diet. The American Academy of Pediatric Dentistry recommends "brushing" your baby's gums with water and a soft infant toothbrush. As your baby gets his first teeth, take care to clean them using an infant toothpaste. Begin semi-independent dental hygiene routines as soon as your child has the motor coordination to brush. Follow up with a more thorough brushing as needed.

 Essential

It is not uncommon for a child with special needs to resist sitting in a chair and letting someone examine his mouth. Check with the nearest children's hospital for a list of dentists who are experienced in working with children or adults with special needs. In some cases, the child may be sedated so that needed work can be completed.

As your child grows and becomes more independent, he may use his own personal calendar. Help him mark the next dental visit by writing the dentist's name and time. You may also add a small tooth drawing or sticker to the date.

Dental checkups are important for lifelong dental care. Most dentists suggest visits twice a year.

Medical

Most teens and young adults should be taught basic medical skills:

BASIC MEDICAL SKILLS

- How to take his temperature with a digital thermometer
- How to read the guidelines for taking an over-the-counter pain reliever
- How to recognize a rash that needs medical attention
- Use of sunscreen and treatment of sunburn
- Treatment of minor cuts and burns
- How to recognize when a cut or burn requires medical attention
- Basic treatment of common illnesses (colds and flu)
- Understanding that medical attention should be sought if in severe pain
- Contacting 9-1-1 in extreme emergency

His cognitive and motor ability will often dictate if your child is ready to assume these responsibilities.

Grooming

Grooming habits impact appearance and, in many cases, overall health. Use a checklist like the following to promote a daily routine:

GROOMING CHECKLIST—NIGHT

- ✓ Select clean clothing for the next day.
- ✓ Check clothing for tears or missing buttons.
- ✓ Iron clothing if wrinkled.
- ✓ Check shoes for dirt or mud.
- ✓ Clean shoes if needed.
- ✓ Put on pajamas.
- ✓ Brush and floss teeth.

GROOMING CHECKLIST—MORNING

✓ Eat breakfast.

✓ Brush and floss teeth.

✓ Wash face and hands.

✓ Comb or brush hair.

✓ Get dressed.

A small checklist can be taped on the adult child's mirror or inside a calendar for quick reference.

Exercise

Help your child establish exercise habits he can follow throughout his life based on his interests and physical ability. Exercise programs may include:

GROUP EXERCISE

- Sports
- Bowling
- Exercise classes
- Activity classes (dance, judo, gymnastics)

INDIVIDUAL EXERCISE

- Walking
- Running
- Bicycling
- Horseback riding (supervised)
- Swimming (supervised)

Your child does not have to compete on a team, but a blend of activity with others and individual exercise is one way to stay on a healthful track. It is human nature to drift away from an exercise schedule that does not include the encouragement of other participants or trainers. A weekly schedule of two to three exercise activities is optimum.

Driving

Whether your child becomes a licensed driver depends on factors that are included in the assessment of all drivers. Drivers who are disabled have learned successful strategies and may use adaptive devices to safely navigate the roads. The Association for Driver Rehabilitation Specialists describes four areas of assessment for potential drivers.

The Rules of the Road

The ability to understand and follow the rules of the road is one factor in assessing potential drivers. Difficulty understanding the rules and following them may result from cognitive delay, memory difficulty, or trouble processing information about the situation at hand.

Visual Acuity

In order to drive, an individual must have sufficient ability to see the driving environment and controls of the motor vehicle. She must have the perception needed to identify other vehicles, pedestrians, and objects in the driving range. In some cases, visual acuity can be corrected with glasses or adapted mirrors in the car.

Attention to the Road

Some potential drivers may understand the rules of the road, but may have significant attention difficulties that impact reaction time. A would-be driver who is easily distracted by the events around her becomes a hazard to herself and others on the road. *Some* individuals with ADHD or ADD have such extreme difficulties maintaining attention that they may not be good candidates for driving. Others are able to maintain sufficient focus through medication or learned strategies.

Some individuals with cerebral palsy also have difficulty maintaining sufficient focus to drive. In addition, the physical limitations of cerebral palsy (and those of spina bifida) can impact use of the legs. Hand controls for gas and brakes and a "spin knob" on the steering wheel may be used to better manage the car.

Reaction to Driving Situations

Disabilities that involve vision, physical movement, comprehension, or information processing can impact the driver's reaction to potentially dangerous situations. If the would-be driver cannot demonstrate reasonable reaction time, she will not be issued a driver's license.

Living Arrangements

Soon after parents come to grips with their child's special needs, they begin to wonder about his future. The question of *where* he will live is one of their important concerns. There are several common options, but the number of arrangements is endless.

Independence

The preferred goal, if at all possible, is to help your child progress to the point where he can live independently. Although this depends on the unique circumstances of the individual, those with some kinds of special needs are more apt to live on their own. Individuals who are deaf, blind, or have a learning disability are likely to develop the strategies needed to live independently, using assistance from outside of the home as needed.

Someone who is deaf might use an interpreter for communication in school, business transactions, and medical or legal appointments. An interpreter, however, does not need to live in the house. A person with ADHD might seek the assistance of a coach to help in organizational skills. Again, that coach would not live in the same house.

 **Question**

Where do adults with disabilities live?
The answer depends on the family structure, type and extent of the disability, and how well the individual can compensate. With learned strategies, education, and adapted equipment, many adults with disabilities lead completely independent lives. Others need support or even total care throughout their lives.

Living with a Relative

In some instances, the individual will live with a relative. When his parents are no longer able to care for him or offer their home as a place to stay, a family member provides the needed housing and day-to-day support. In this model, the provider is often (but not always) a sibling.

HCB Programs

In the past, an individual who was mentally retarded might live at home or in a nursing home or institution. A home and community-based program (HCB) provides services to assist the individual in living in the community. He may live in a choice of settings based on his needs: the individual's home, group home, or Intermediate Care Facility for the Mentally Retarded (ICF/MR). In some cases, the most appropriate living arrangement continues to be an institution, nursing home, or qualifying hospital.

The Mental Retardation or Developmental Disabilities Living (MR/DD Living) website (*www.mrddliving.org*) lists the following services of HCB programs:

- Case management
- Homemaker
- Home health aide services

- Personal care services
- Adult day care
- Habilitation
- Respite care

The goal is for the individual to live in an environment where he is able to function as independently as possible, while receiving the benefit of socialization from others in the community. In order to do this, some support services may be needed. The amount of support depends on the individual's needs and whether it is a reasonable use of available funding.

Homemaking Skills

Homemaking skills allow the individual to live as independently as possible whether living at home, in an ICF/MR, or in a group home. Even when assistance is provided through an HCB program, independence in homemaking skills is the goal. Involving your child in these activities as soon as she is ready will help prepare her for life as an adult.

Food Preparation

Perhaps your child lives where she prepares her own meals. Perhaps she lives with others or is living with your family. Strive to teach her some food preparation skills to boost her independence and self-confidence.

Make a shopping list and include the items needed from each food group. Fresh fruits and vegetables require little preparation. For "dishes" that don't require cooking from scratch, prepackaged, microwaveable foods and make-it-from-the-box items are plentiful. Teach your child these kitchen basics:

- Safe food handling
- Oven and stove settings
- Handling of hot pans
- Measurements (cup, tablespoon, teaspoon, fractions)
- Cooking vocabulary (mix/stir, boil, bake, chop, freeze, drain, refrigerate after opening)
- Kitchen clean up

Teach cooking skills in this order: no-cook snacks, heat-up foods, "box" items (prepared with only a few steps), and simple recipes.

Clothes

Basic laundry skills (sorting, washing, drying, and folding) are necessary life skills. Your adult child should also understand how to determine if an item is "dry clean only." Checking for stains, tears, and missing buttons are additional needed skills. If your child has the necessary fine motor skills, teach her how to sew on a button. Ironing is not as critical as a few years ago because of modern fabrics and better clothes dryers, but some items still need that attention.

Knowing which clothing to wear is as important as knowing how to care for clothing. Your adult child should understand dressing for the weather. She should also understand appropriate clothing for common events: work, casual, and formal.

Being able to match clothes is another socially expected skill. If your child is color blind or does not seem to understand whether clothing items match, give her some assistance. Sew a small, colored tag inside the shirts and pants that go together. Instead of labeling one-to-one pairs (shirt-pants), you might use the same color of tag in several shirts and pants, indicating that the items could be mixed-and-matched.

Other Household Responsibilities

Establish a cleaning schedule for your child. It should include everyday tasks: making her bed, picking up, washing dishes, taking out the trash. It should also include jobs that are less frequent, but done routinely (dusting, vacuuming, cleaning the bathroom, doing laundry, washing windows). If your child has yard work responsibilities (grass cutting, trimming, sweeping the sidewalks and porches, gardening, raking leaves), they should be taught on a routine as well.

Finances

In addition to basic money skills (Chapter 3), your child will need to learn fundamental money management. Some individuals will live independently as adults and make all of their own money decisions. Many (living at home or in a group-home setting in the community) need to budget personal expenses, but not housing costs.

Money Management Assistant

Regardless of the living arrangement, your child may benefit from a money management assistant. A money management assistant may be:

- Parent or other relative
- Designated worker in group home
- Vocational rehabilitation counselor

Money management assistant is not a formal job title. Rather, it is someone who can answer financial questions, help create a budget, and offer general advice on money.

Budget for Independent Living

If your child is going to live independently, he will need to budget for "household" expenses. If he lives in an apartment, some of the items may already be included in his rent. The household budget may include some or all of the following:

HOUSEHOLD BUDGET
- ✓ Savings
- ✓ Rent or house payment
- ✓ Gas and electricity
- ✓ Water
- ✓ Garbage

✓ Insurance
✓ Furnishings (furniture, linens, kitchenware)
✓ Emergency funds
✓ Food
✓ Personal expenses

As with any budget, funds are not unlimited. Work with your child to manage the money in his budget so that all of the necessities are covered and extras are provided for within reason. Some amounts of money, such as savings, should accumulate over time.

Personal Expense Budget

Every individual needs a personal expense budget. Again, a money management assistant can help set up the amounts and monitor whether or not the budget is followed and if adjustments should be made. A personal expense budget plan may look like the following:

PERSONAL EXPENSE BUDGET

✓ Toiletries (soap, shampoo, hair spray, razors, shaving cream, toothpaste, toothbrush)
✓ Medical supplies (thermometer, pain relievers, Band-Aids, antiseptic, sunscreen)
✓ Special equipment not funded by outside source
✓ Medical and dental care
✓ Clothing
✓ Laundry (soap, dryer sheets, washer/dryer money)
✓ Transportation (including car insurance)
✓ Entertainment
✓ Recreation
✓ Leisure travel

Wants and Needs

Your child will need to distinguish between wants and needs. Perhaps your child loves going to baseball games. He may not be able to attend every game, but by saving a small amount regularly in an entertainment fund, he will be able to afford a trip to the game periodically.

There are also different ways to plan purchases in each area. A pair of blue jeans can cost one amount at a family clothing store and a completely different amount at a popular teen/young adult clothing store. Work with your child to budget and live within his means. Obtaining pricier items can be a savings goal, added to a gift wish list, or something to purchase when he is making a little more money.

Applications and Forms

Paperwork abounds wherever you go. Adequate life skills include knowing how to fill out basic forms and the communication skills to ask for needed help. Most applications and forms fall into a few general categories and use repetitive information. Job applications and forms (Chapter 19) may vary greatly in appearance, but they also call for basically the same information.

 Fact

Some things apply to all forms. *All* forms will require name, address, phone, and e-mail. Knowing how to provide this basic information is a life skill that will be used frequently. Some forms will ask for additional information. The individual should print clearly, include only the requested information, and ask for assistance as needed in completing the forms.

Housing forms are used for group homes, rental property, and college dorms. Typically these forms fall into four categories: applications, rental contracts, damage reports, and maintenance requests.

When completing a damage report or a maintenance request, it is important to use clear, short sentences or phrases to explain. The answers to the following questions will usually supply the needed information:

- What is the problem? (leaking faucet, broken lock, no heat)
- Where is the problem? (apartment number and room—perhaps the kitchen/the college room number)
- When is the form filled out? (date)
- Who completed the form? (name)
- How can you be contacted? (phone number and e-mail)

Medical forms ask the basic identifying information (name, address, phone number) that your child has already learned. Additional information may include:

- Insurance, Medicare, or Medicaid information
- Names of contacts in case of emergency
- Immunization history
- Personal and family medical history
- Reason for office visit

Most of the above information can be kept on a medical information sheet, which the individual can take to doctor's appointments.

In many cases, a family member or group home worker should attend the appointment to assist with paperwork and to listen to follow-up and care recommendations. If medication is prescribed, a chart for dosage and times may be created, or (according to the individual's needs) the medication intake can be monitored by a family member or group home worker.

Emergency forms (kept on file by schools and employers) are much briefer. They might include:

- Name
- Address
- Phone number
- Email address
- Allergies
- Medications
- Insurance/Medicare/Medicaid information
- Name of people to contact in case of emergency
- Hospital preference

One approach to foster your child's independence in using forms is to create master sheets: medical, financial, work, and housing. Divide each sheet into appropriate sections with titles. Then the sheets can be used for quick reference to fill out most forms.

Resources

Government and private organizations and agencies can be important resources for the young adult. Understanding who can help and how to access that assistance is an important step to independence and confidence.

Community Agencies

Many community agencies (not only those established to serve individuals with special needs) offer assistance, often at no charge. Once contact has been made, add a resource page to the young adult's notebook for future reference.

COMMUNITY RESOURCES
- Food pantry
- County health department
- WIC program (*supplemental nutrition assistance to women, infants and children*)

- Motor vehicle department
- Women's crisis center
- Salvation Army
- Early childhood intervention services
- County housing authority
- Social Security
- Unemployment office
- Utility offices

Create a contact log for each agency that has been accessed. Include the date, name of the contact, and notes about information or requests made of the office.

Specialized Agencies

Some agencies in the community deal primarily with individuals with disabilities as well as making the community aware of their abilities and needs. These agencies should also be included in the individual resource book.

The Division of Vocational Rehabilitation (Chapters 18 and 19) provides counseling, training, and various types of funding to qualified individuals. The agency's goal is to assist individuals in becoming as independent as possible and to be working, contributing members of society. Individual aptitude, interests, and special needs are considered in developing each client's plan.

Organizations for specific disabilities offer detailed information about the disability and how it can impact areas of life. This information can be helpful when explaining special needs to family members and employers. Often, organization websites include current research and best practice information. The sites may list strategies for success and links for related products.

Advocacy groups (see Chapter 21) may be connected to an organization for a specific disability. They may be offices that house professionals and volunteers who focus on different areas of special need (hearing, vision, learning disabilities, autism, developmental delay, traumatic brain injury, or mental illness) and serve a geographic area. The young adult establishing independence can get information, support, and referral to other resources through an advocacy group.

ADA and Other Disability-Related Legislation

The U.S. Department of Justice publication, *A Guide to Disability Rights Laws,* outlines legislation regarding the law specific to those who are disabled or those who employ or serve those individuals with a disability. The entire text of each section of this booklet can be read online and includes:

A GUIDE TO DISABILITY RIGHTS LAWS
- Americans with Disabilities Act
- Telecommunications Act
- Fair Housing Act
- Air Carrier Access Act
- Voting Accessibility for the Elderly and Handicapped Act
- National Voter Registration Act
- Civil Rights of Institutionalized Persons Act
- Individuals with Disabilities Education Act
- Rehabilitation Act
- Architectural Barriers Act
- General Sources of Disability Rights Information
- Statute Citations

Perhaps the most widely known are the Individual with Disabilities Act (IDEA—Chapter 11) and the Americans with Disabilities Act (ADA).

The Americans with Disability Act includes four titles:

- **ADA Title I:** Employment

- **ADA Title II:** State and Local Government Activities (including Public Transportation)
- **ADA Title III:** Public Accommodations
- **ADA Title IV:** Telecommunication Relay Services

 Fact

The Fair Housing Act protects against discrimination in housing based on disability. It allows renters to have guide dogs when the property is otherwise off-limits to pets. It also allows renters to make needed physical accommodations to their apartment or home. New buildings that will be rented as four or more units must have accessible doors, kitchens, bathrooms, and common areas.

Advocacy groups and organizations for specific disabilities can provide you with information on how U.S. law protects the rights of the individual with a disability. They can also guide you in ways to remedy situations where the law is not followed.

CHAPTER 18

Postsecondary Education

From the time your child is born, you will plan for his future. Is your child prepared to face the adult world? How will your child's adult world look? Further education, job training, life skills, finances, and personal independence will be continuing concerns. Postsecondary education can be part of the answer to your child's preparation by providing shelter workshop training, community on-the-job training, a trade school program, or a community college or college degree. A lifetime of educational goals and strategies can help guide your child in the postsecondary choice that is right for him.

Individual Choices

What happens after high school depends on the individual, whether or not she has a disability, and the nature of that disability. Some students are ready to jump into the work world unassisted. For some, the transition to some type of supported employment is logical. Others seek ongoing training or education to pursue a particular job.

Interests and Aptitudes

The postsecondary season of a student's educational career may be the first time that she can really choose to study what interests her. High schools do offer career and technical programs (some including community work placement for a portion of the school day) for qualified students. Elective courses (music, art, home economics, business, technical, and IT) are also offered for students completing a traditional high school track. However, postsecondary education focuses solely on a particular field of study in preparation for the work world. An individual who wants to become a hairstylist will study the needed information and skills to pursue that work when attending cosmetology school. Similarly, the individual who wants to become a teacher will learn about child development and sound practices in education as she attends a teacher preparation program in college.

 Alert

In order for your student to receive appropriate accommodations for any of the College Board tests (PSAT/NMSQT, SAT Reasoning and Subject Tests, or AP—Advanced Placement Tests) she must complete a Student Eligibility Form. The form includes documentation of the disability, diagnosis, and functional limitations, and must be approved before accommodations can be made.

Aptitude Testing

Information from your student's triennial re-evaluations for special education services will provide some information on his aptitudes. Aptitude testing given to all high school students will offer additional information on fields of work which may be of interest as well. Too often, students consider only a small group of jobs as options. However, not everyone becomes a teacher, a waitress, or a store clerk. Aptitude testing can provide a previously unconsidered (and maybe unknown) list of careers or career areas for further exploration. Some areas or jobs listed may not be of interest to the student. Certainly it is possible for someone to have natural ability in an area that does not interest her. And certainly that would not be an area to pursue for future job training.

Many students take the Preliminary SAT (PSAT) or National Merit Scholarship Qualifying Test (NMSQT) as a requirement early in their high school career. According to the College Board website, the PSAT/NMSQT measures critical reading skills, math problem-solving skills, and writing skills. The test offers students a means "to receive feedback on . . . strengths and weaknesses on skills necessary for college study." The test is co-sponored by the National Merit Scholarship Corporation and allows students to be considered for merit-based scholarships. Students who are seriously considering college will go on to take the SAT or ACT to determine college acceptance.

 Fact

According to their website, the ACT, which also provides college entrance examinations, offers three kinds of services for students with disabilities: "testing with accommodations, testing with additional time (50 percent), and testing with alternate test formats." An alternate test format might be a Braille test for a student who is blind. The ACT requires the student to document her disability prior to being given accommodations.

Impact of the Disability

The individual's interests and aptitudes may be a good fit for her chosen profession regardless of her disability. The student who is a visual learner and is interested in mechanical things, for example, may be a good candidate for a trade school, specializing in auto mechanics, heating and cooling services, computer installation, or basic electrical engineering. In other cases the disability can make a career goal difficult, and in some cases, impossible. The student with mechanical interests who also has low vision might not be the best candidate for the programs of study listed above.

Additional Testing Through Agencies

The Division of Vocational Rehabilitation, sheltered workshop, and supported employment programs (all often under the umbrella of VR) can also evaluate a student's aptitude for job fields or even specific positions. An occupational therapist in such a program might evaluate a client's fine motor ability to perform a specific job, offering ideas for strategies and accommodations to help her succeed. In some cases, the OT might suggest a different position that would be better suited to the client's interests, aptitude, and physical ability.

Transition Plans

The move from high school to work, trade school, or college does not just happen. Formal planning will begin with your student's IEP team around the time he enters high school. IDEA 2004 states that age sixteen is the milestone when the school district must include a *Transition Plan* in a student's IEP, although it is permissible for a transition plan to be started earlier.

Begin to talk with your child about his personal goals for the future long before the mandatory transition meetings. A well-developed plan that reflects your child's interests and goals will not come together in a short meeting around a table. Take time to discuss and explore options with your child.

Transition Plan Participants

In most cases, the IEP team servicing a student with a disability involves a fairly large group of people. Transition plan participants can also make up a fairly large group. The group might include: a special education teacher, regular education teacher, school counselor, Vocational Rehabilitation counselor, parents, orientation and mobility specialist, audiologist, interpreter, psychologist, and above all, the student. The key is that one planning group is handing over the planning to the group that will work with the student after high school. The student leads this transition plan as his personal interests and goals are addressed in preparation for his life as an adult.

Focus of the Transition Plan

The transition plan for a student with a disability is focused on educational services that will assist him in reaching or continuing to work toward his post–high school goals. These goals might include ongoing education, employment, involvement in community activities, and living arrangements. A transition plan is designed and implemented for each student individually regardless of whether he will receive a high school diploma or a high school certificate of completion.

Technical and Trade Schools

Some students receive adequate trade school instruction during the high school years to enter immediately into employment. Others continue in a formal, postsecondary trade school to learn about other career fields, or to obtain a certificate or license that can increase employment opportunities and bring a higher wage.

Vocations

The vocations addressed in trade schools vary greatly from hands-on trades such as small-engine repair and carpentry to business school programs. Again, the program chosen should take into account the student's aptitudes, interests, and disability. A disability should not define what the individual does, but needed accommodations and strategies should be considered before making an educational and career choice. Does your student feel comfortable and confident about the needed accommodations and strategies for a particular vocation? If not, perhaps another kind of employment should be considered.

More Consideration

Trade school programs vary in length from a few months to several years. Some offer training in the evenings to accommodate individuals who are working during the day. Funding may be available from Vocational Rehabilitation for a client to attend a trade school. Because funding is limited and is awarded after individual consideration, it is best to begin work with VR early to ensure timely consideration for available funds.

Trade Schools Specific to Certain Disabilities

Like public high schools, some residential schools have a vocational track to prepare high school students for the work world. This is often the case in residential schools for the deaf, blind, developmentally delayed, or emotionally disturbed. The focus of these programs is work-related skills and often includes an actual work experience on campus or in the community.

 Fact

In some cases, only short-term training is needed for employees. Some jobs provide on-the-job training. Some employees with disabilities receive additional, specialized training from a job coach as a part of a supported employment program. Still others work in sheltered workshops with repetitive tasks that are completed under supervision (see Chapter 19).

At the postsecondary level, students with certain disabilities may attend a technical school that employs specialized staff and methods to train the students. An example is the National Technical Institute for the Deaf in Rochester, New York, which is a college of the Rochester Institute of Technology.

Community College

One postsecondary option is community college. Community colleges are strategically located to provide a college within easy commuting range.

The community college student population can be divided into several broad categories:

- Students who choose to pay less for the first years of school by living at home. They plan to transfer to a four-year college or university beginning their sophomore or junior year of college.
- Students working toward an associate's degree.
- Students who are taking a few classes and trying to establish their educational goals.
- Married students and single parents. Many are taking classes part-time or in the evening.
- Students with a special need who are seeing if college is right for them.

There are many benefits to the student with a disability in this kind of postsecondary program.

Testing and Developmental Classes

To enter most community colleges (even for a summer course) students are required to provide one of the following:

- Scores from the ACT or SAT college tests.
- A transcript of previous college coursework.
- Current college enrollment information. This would be the case for a student who is enrolled in a four-year college or university but would like to take community college classes during the summer.

- Complete a college skills/placement test on the community college campus.

If no other documentation is provided, the student will take the community college skills/placement test to determine the student's knowledge of math, Reading, and English.

 Alert

> Prior to the student's scheduled test, she should contact the testing office or the office that provides support services for students with disabilities to request needed accommodations. Accommodations for such testing might include an interpreter for the deaf or a reader for a student with a learning disability. Readers are not used for the Reading tests.

If her scores fall below a specified level, she will be required to take *developmental courses* to boost her skills in these subjects and therefore increase her chances for success in college coursework. Otherwise, the student may be placed in college-level coursework to begin.

If a student is required to take developmental courses, those credits and grades will count toward her community college Grade Point Average (GPA). They will not, however, count as degree requirements. A student who tests into a developmental English course will still have to take the English course requirements for her degree in addition to the developmental English coursework.

Support Services

Any college or university receiving money from the government is required to offer support services for students with disabilities. The services a student can use depend on the documented needs of the student. (See College—Educational Accommodations later for more information.)

Other Benefits

Many students with disabilities recognize additional benefits of attending a community college. Many live in apartments and enjoy independence that they did not have as a high school student.

Socialization is another benefit of community college. Students have the opportunity to meet nondisabled adults from across the community. Often, the group of peers with the same disability is larger than it was in high school as multiple schools feed into the community college.

Increased contact with others with similar needs promotes opportunities for campus and community awareness. Many community colleges host a Disability Awareness Day for this purpose.

Associate's Degrees

Some students will be able to reach their career goals with an associate's degree. An associate's degree can be appealing because it can be obtained in two years and allows the student to enter the workforce quickly. Many certificate programs also are available for completion in one year if the student is attending full-time.

Transfer Considerations

Many students feel that it's logical to attend a community college, receive an associate's degree, and then transfer to a four-year college or university. In some instances, students (and their families) can save money if the student lives at home the first two years, and only pays for housing for the remaining two years. Often community college campuses are small, and students may get more personal attention from community college faculty and staff.

There are considerations in transferring from a community college to a four-year institution. Some general education classes do not transfer. It seems like a course in civilization would be recognized at any postsecondary institution, but that is not necessarily the case. It is quite possible for a student to earn an associate's degree only to find that some of his courses will not transfer to a four-year institution.

 **Essential**

There are "safe courses" to take at a community college. Included in this list are developmental classes (which are not considered to be degree requirements), freshman-level English classes, psychology, and sociology. To be sure, talk directly with an academic advisor from your student's four-year college or university.

The safest way to ensure that course credit will transfer from a community college to a four-year college or university is to work directly with an academic advisor from the four-year institution. Although academic advisors at community colleges have information about many four-year programs, information changes quickly. They may not be aware if a policy has changed.

College

Students who have the academic ability may decide to attend a four-year college program. Although accommodations are available to students with documented disabilities, the college-age student should also have appropriate classroom and study strategies in order to be successful in college.

Educational Accommodations

It is the student's responsibility to advise the college or university of his disability if he is interested in receiving appropriate educational accommodations. Certainly it is possible for a college student to have a disability that does not impact his education, or a disability for which he has adequate strategies to be successful without additional accommodations.

A student who has mild cerebral palsy, walking with Canadian crutches, may not need educational accommodations. (Because of ADA, the college would already have doors that could be opened with a button and elevators, removing any barrier to building accessibility.)

A student with low vision may already have sufficient support from using a tripod magnifier to read textbooks and exams. Enlarging the print on a computer could be accomplished with the click of a button. Perhaps this student would not need further accommodations.

Each student is, however, an individual with unique needs. Many students will request educational accommodations from their college. These accommodations might include:

- Enlarged print handouts
- Reader services (for visually impaired students as well as those with a learning disability)
- Writer services (an individual to whom the student dictates in-class written work and essay exams)
- Interpreter for the deaf
- Note taker

Students may also use other accommodations that would not necessarily be provided by the college, such as textbooks on tape.

Housing Considerations

The other main area of accommodation for college students is living accommodations. Typically this is handled by staff in the housing office as opposed to the office that coordinates classroom services.

Students needing living accommodation include some with physical impairments, some with visual impairments, and those who use a service dog.

Funding

Most families are concerned about the cost of a college education. Students with a disability have a number of options in the search for college funding:

- Traditional, merit-based scholarships
- Scholarships based on an area of talent (sports, debate, etc.)
- Scholarships based on ethnicity
- Scholarships based on community involvement
- Traditional student loans
- Supplemental Security Income (SSI)
- Funding from the Division of Vocational Rehabilitation or the Rehabilitation Services for the Blind
- Scholarships awarded to students with a particular disability

In some cases, a college student with a disability who also works may continue to be eligible for SSI with documentation that his earnings are being used to pay for his college expenses. This program is called PASS (Plan for Achieving Self-Support) and is decided on an individual basis.

The HEATH Resource Center offers online and print material to assist the college student with a disability in finding financial assistance (*www.heath.gwu.edu*).

CHAPTER 19

Getting a Job

Most likely, at some point your teen or adult child will look for a job. Perhaps it will be a part-time job during high school or college. Perhaps it will be a professional job after she completes formal schooling. Perhaps it will be a more guided beginning in a sheltered workshop or supported employment environment. Certain basic skills and practices apply for each situation. Acquiring the appropriate education or training, role-playing best workplace practices, and getting involved with the right agencies will be important to her success.

Agencies to Know

There is no law that prevents your child from beating the bushes to find employment just like his siblings. Getting a job on his own would be a great boost to his confidence, as well it should be. However, if his disability is severe or if he has extreme communication needs, your child may benefit from the assistance of an agency.

Social Security Administration

Some children receive Supplemental Security Income their entire lives because of the severity of their disabilities. (See Chapter 6.) Some who did not qualify for SSI as young children because of family income may be eligible when they turn eighteen years of age. Check with the Social Security Office to see if your child qualifies for any funding. Note that although your child may qualify for SSI, he can still work. His income will affect the amount of SSI he receives.

 Fact

The Americans with Disabilities Amendments Act (2008) safeguards against employment discrimination based on disability (that "substantially limits a major life activity"). The Act applies to places of work with more than fifteen employees, and covers reasonable physical accommodations, training modifications, and job placement. The Act addresses fair hiring and treatment on the job, but does not guarantee employment.

Division of Vocational Rehabilitation (VR)

The Rehabilitation Services Administration is a government agency that oversees some types of job training, independent living centers, supported employment, and the protection of individual rights of the disabled. The Rehabilitation Services Administration is under the U.S. Office of Special Education and Rehabilitation Services. Its mission statement reads: "To provide leadership to achieve full integration and participation in society of people with disabilities by ensuring equal opportunity and access to, and excellence in, education, employment and community living."

Individuals are taken into state Vocational Rehabilitation programs (often referred to as Voc Rehab, VR, or DORS [Division of Vocational Rehabilitation]) based on the severity of their need. Severe physical needs, mental disabilities, or the extreme communication needs of most deaf people are among some of the first to be considered. Funding for various training and supports is given to individuals based on need.

Through VR an individual might be eligible for a range of services, from training for a skilled job to college funding. A counselor within the VR program works with qualified individuals to attain independent living and work goals.

 Essential

> The Division of Rehabilitation Services offers programs and services to transition youth (ages fourteen to twenty-four) into careers or post-secondary education. These high school/high tech (HS/HT) programs include "school-based preparatory experiences, career preparation and work-based learning experiences, youth development and leadership, connecting activities, and family involvement and support."

Personal Purpose

One aspect of job success is personal purpose. A job does not have to be well known or pay big bucks to fulfill the worker's sense of personal purpose or satisfaction. The individual who is a school crossing guard, for example, does not have a high-profile position (except to the children and families who benefit from her services). She certainly does not earn a large salary. Her personal purpose may be enough for her to continue with this job if she enjoys children. She understands the importance of her role in society by helping children safely cross the street on the way to their destinations.

Your child will develop her own concept of personal purpose based on several factors. Especially at the beginning of her work life, she will look to you for input on what jobs are meaningful and serve a purpose in society, and what jobs you might find trivial. Although she may not verbally ask for your input, she will be watching to see your response. The individual whose family is positive and supportive about her work in the mall food court will maintain the same positive attitude and healthy self-concept. In the long run, she will develop her own thinking about jobs. If the job fits her aptitude and interests as well as her abilities, she will find it fulfilling.

Aptitude

Regardless of disability or special need, each person is born with certain aptitudes or talents. Often (but not always) those aptitudes are the things that a person most enjoys doing—probably in part because those are the tasks that come easily. There are several general categories of aptitude:

- Mechanical aptitude is evidenced in working with or repairing machines. An individual with mechanical aptitude might work with cars, electrical systems, plumbing, or even computer installation or computer hardware (system) maintenance.
- Some individuals have an aptitude for other kinds of work with their hands. These workers enjoy carpentry, metalwork, sewing, baking, and crafts.
- Other individuals have more aptitude for working with people. They are drawn to work with children, assisting the elderly, sales, and waitressing.
- Some people are very analytic. Some have an aptitude for math and science.
- Some are artistic and have an aptitude for music, dance, acting, or other forms of fine art.

 Fact

Self-employment is a growing trend across all populations. This is also true for individuals with disabilities. Being self-employed sidesteps frustrating application and hiring situations, but the total responsibility of securing work is then obviously on the individual. State Vocational Rehabilitation programs have some provisions for assisting individuals in developing self-employment plans.

Aptitude is also evidenced by the student's preference for activities and classes. Most students can easily identify what they like and dislike. Exploring the multitude of work choices is a little harder.

Most students think they only have a handful of options. They are the careers they see in action every day: teacher, mechanic, doctor, restaurant worker, salesman, fireman, policemen, and so on. In reality, there are many other interesting jobs that people do not think about. For example, who creates popular video games or the toys that come in fast food meals? Who creates the displays in museums and store windows? Who works at the airport with international travelers?

Aptitude tests are often given in high school and by vocational counselors. These tests present students with choices: *Would you rather* _____ *(activity A) or* _____ *(activity B)?* The result is a report of aptitudes and interests as well as some related careers.

Ability

Sometimes disabilities seem to conflict with aptitude, and the disability at least partially inhibits the full expression of the aptitude. An example is the student with ADHD who has an aptitude in math. She can do math problems with little effort when she stays focused on what the problem is asking and follows through with the needed computation. Often, though, she may be distracted from paying attention to the details of the problem, or she may get impatient with the amount of time needed to complete all of the steps. Her aptitude in math is overshadowed by her disability.

One key to your child's career success is to find a job that she enjoys and can do well. This is not to say that a disability should close the door to a desired career, but there should be a workable relationship between her aptitude and her disability. An individual who is deaf may have a knack at motivating others. She develops her skills at motivational speaking. She has speaking engagements at many events for the deaf, but she would like to broaden the scope of her speaking. Through the use of an interpreter she is able to speak to any group of people. She has found a workable relationship between her aptitude and her disability by using a strategy to get around her hearing loss.

Some strategies that are used to work around a disability include assistive technology, time management and planning, communication devices, orthopedic equipment, services of other individuals (interpreter, physical assistant, mobility or orientation guide), and the use of assistive dogs.

Education and Training

Every job requires some type of training. Perhaps your child has a job walking the neighbor's dog. Your child will be told how often and how far to walk the dog, and whether it should have breaks along the way. He also will be told what to do if approaching another dog and its owner. But not all job training is that simple. The training and education needed for a job might range from on-the-job instruction to multiple college degrees.

On-the-Job Training

Some jobs provide training on the job. Every job provides some type of orientation to the specific position, but true on-the-job training is all-inclusive. Some jobs that offer such training include:

- Waiting tables
- Cook
- Busboy
- Janitor
- Sales clerk

- Receptionist
- Some child care positions
- Groundskeeper
- Bus driver

Your child may be hired for work that offers on-the-job training to all employees. He may be part of a supported work program in which a job coach provides additional, specialized on-the-job training. An example would be a worker with a cognitive delay who would need straightforward instruction and detailed feedback for the required work tasks. Some workers may require specialized instruction in addition to job training. A worker who is visually impaired may need orientation and mobility training.

Sheltered Workshops

If the worker is part of a sheltered workshop, he will receive ongoing on-the-job training. Supervisors and trainers are a part of this work model, where the tasks are easily mastered by the workers and are completed in an environment of workers who are predominantly disabled.

Trade Schools and Certification Programs

Some jobs require some training, but not a college degree program. Examples of jobs that require this level of education and training include:

- Electrician
- Plumber
- Auto mechanic
- Hairstylist
- Real estate agent
- Insurance agent
- Dental hygienist
- Lab technician
- X-ray technician
- Emergency medical technician
- Police officer
- Firefighter

Training for these jobs might be in a trade school, short-term training program, or a certificate program offered by a community college.

College

Some jobs require an associate's degree, bachelor's degree, or higher levels of college work. Without a degree and professional license or certificate in the field, these jobs cannot be obtained. The following are basic skills indicating success in most college programs:

- Written and oral communication ability (The student may communicate through an interpreter if he is deaf or with assistive technology if he has a physical impairment.)
- Understanding of program concepts (A student with a learning disability may need books in audio format, but he should be able to grasp the ideas presented on the tapes.)
- Ability to attend to a task (The student may use strategies to break up study tasks and to complete assignments.)
- Perseverance in long-range goals (The student should be able to work toward a goal that will last several years.)

Reasonable accommodations are available to students with various disabilities to provide support to complete the programs.

Applications and Forms

Unless your child is mowing the neighbor's lawn or babysitting with their children, applications and forms will be a necessary part of getting a job. Although they can seem complicated, most employment applications and new hire forms have the same basic information, and often the paperwork can be completed at home and returned to the employer.

There are ways to practice filling out applications ahead of time or to at least talk through them. Check with your child's teacher for sample applications. Your child should have the following basic information when she goes to fill out applications:

- Full name
- Address
- Length of time at the address
- Phone number (home and cell)
- Social security number
- Names and contact information for three references

- Information about previous employment (name of contact, length of time at that job)
- Days and times available for work

Many employers offer (if not require) online applications. If they can be retrieved on your home computer, online applications offer two main benefits. They can be filled out at your child's pace with your support, and they can be used to practice general application skills without submitting them.

The work world is a place of forms and more forms. When your child is first hired she will be expected to fill out the same kinds of forms that you filled out for your employer. There are several ways to handle complicated paperwork:

- Arrange a time that you can go with your child to complete the W-4 form, insurance forms, and other miscellaneous documents.
- Have your child ask if she can take the needed paperwork home and then return it completed.
- Write down the basic information she might need and send it with her.

The W-4 is always the tricky one. Know how to fill it out based on your family's tax information.

The Interview

Most jobs require some type of an interview. Talk with your child about the purpose of the interview. The employer wants to get to know him and to see how he interacts with other people. The employer wants to see his attitude and ask him questions about "what if" situations. Your child should be aware that sometimes an interview happens right on the spot as soon as he fills out the application, and other times interviews are scheduled much like an appointment. Sometimes more than one person will be conducting the interview.

Explain the importance of appearance to your child. An interview is a time to look *well kept*. It is not necessary to dress in the popular clothing of his peer group (unless the interview is to work in a clothing store). Rather, it is a time to appear neat and to wear semi-dressy clothing. Your child's appearance will communicate (without words) that this job is important and that he wants to make a good impression.

Practice interview talk with your child. Get both parents, or a parent and working sibling, involved. One can role-play as the potential employer. The other can be the one being interviewed. Act out an interview and let your child see how it is done. If time allows, also act out a poor interview. Talk with your child about what was done correctly and what was not. Then let your child take a turn being interviewed.

This practice will help your child predict the kind of questions that might be asked. He will be comfortable giving appropriate, focused answers because he has experience with interview talk.

Encourage your child to end the interview conversation with three points:

- Thank the potential employer for the interview.
- Affirm that he is interested in the position.
- Ask what happens next

 Essential

If your child is applying for a professional job, a follow-up letter is always in good taste. In that situation, your child should include the three points in a clear, concise letter. With the convenience of computers, he can create such a letter and save it to use with various potential employers.

Many applicants fill out the forms, go to interviews, and then go home and wait by the phone. Many of those applicants do not get the positions because they do not follow up. Encourage your child to follow up with a phone call or an e-mail a reasonable time after the interview.

Job Behavior and Attitude

Once your child is hired, she will be evaluated by the same standards as other employees. Granted, the employer should make necessary allowance for her disability. It is impossible for a cashier who uses a wheelchair to lift boxes in order to stock her checkout aisle. In all other regards, your child is an employee and should use the best work practices.

Punctuality and Attendance

Most workplaces have an expected schedule for their employees. In some workplaces, a new schedule is posted for each week. Make sure that your child understands her schedule and the fact that it is her responsibility to know when she is scheduled to work.

Review the employer guidelines for absenteeism with your child. Here are some policy points that your child should understand:

- Which conditions require absence or prevent returning to work (temperature, rash, lice, pinkeye, other illnesses)
- Personal discretion on work absence
- Reporting an absence
- When a doctor's note might be required
- How absence affects pay
- Personal days, bereavement days, and vacation

Punctuality is another attendance practice that your child should understand. Discuss an appropriate time to get to work.

Typically, an employee should arrive ten to fifteen minutes before her shift begins.

Clothes and Appearance

Discuss appropriate personal appearance for work. Discuss this checklist with your child as it fits her job:

- ✓ Length of hair
- ✓ Jewelry and body piercings
- ✓ Tattoos
- ✓ Makeup and fingernails
- ✓ Uniform requirement
- ✓ Dress code
- ✓ Care of work clothing

You may be able to spring for some of your child's initial work clothing, but talk with her about building her wardrobe. Will she budget a portion of each check for purchasing work clothing? Where will she purchase the clothing? The most popular clothing store may not be financially practical or may not offer the right type of clothes. Sometimes a uniform fee (including a laundry fee for the uniform) is required or routinely deducted from paychecks.

Professional Courtesy

Talk with your child about professional courtesy to her supervisors, coworkers, and customers. Each should be treated with respect.

Although the supervisors' directions should be followed, there should be a level of appropriateness. If the requests are not work-related and cross the line to some type of sexual harassment, it is important that your child understands how to report it. Depending on the communication skills of your child, you may encourage her to talk with you first.

Coworkers should be respected and should show respect in return. Your child should demonstrate and expect teamwork. Talk with your child about following through on the supervisor's requests. Coworkers are not (for the most part) supervisors. Your child should not be concerned with following their directions.

If your child is working with the public, she will need to learn people skills. As a representative of the company or business, she will need to put her best foot forward. In general, having a positive attitude and reporting confrontations to a supervisor are wise.

Regardless of who your child is talking with, she should be aware of professional conversation. Here is a checklist to guide her:

- ✓ Is it about work?
- ✓ Is it spreading a rumor?
- ✓ Is it complaining to the wrong person?
- ✓ Am I sharing private, personal information?
- ✓ Have I talked too long about something?
- ✓ Am I keeping others from getting their work done?

In some instances, it may be helpful to role-play some upsetting or recurring work situations. Help her brainstorm some automatic answers for difficult situations so she is not put on the spot.

Workplace Ethics

Your child has been hired as a trusted employee. Talk with her about the areas where her employer is counting on her.

If your child works in a fast food restaurant, she will have access to food, drinks, supplies, and possibly cash. Usually working in a restaurant means a free or discounted meal, but it does not mean additional food for your child or her friends. Sometimes it is easy to think "since I work here I have the authority to make those calls," but that is not the case.

If your child works in a business or office, supplies might seem free for the taking. She would not walk into a store and steal something, but it may seem okay in an office setting because the item is provided for employees. She should understand that the items (stamps, envelopes, paper, pen, etc.) are provided to employees—for them to use in their work, not for personal use.

Perhaps your child's job involves a cleaning service to businesses or offices after hours. Perhaps no one is onsite to supervise how the work is done. No one is there to see that all of the work is completed or completed as requested. Does the recycled paper end up in the regular dumpster? Are the carpets really vacuumed every evening?

There is another aspect of working in an unsupervised setting—breaks. Without an onsite supervisor during the work shift, it can be tempting to take longer or more frequent breaks. Even if not taking a break, a cell phone can provide distraction from getting the tasks completed.

Work Programs

Some adult children are best suited for a work program that will assist them with their unique needs. The Division of Vocational Rehabilitation, or Voc Rehab or VR, is again the first stop for work program information. Two kinds of programs that the Voc Rehab works with are sheltered workshops and supported employment.

Sheltered workshops employ individuals with disabilities and those who are disadvantaged. They are given the necessary on-the-job training and supervised by staff onsite. Often the work involves repetitive tasks such as packing or collating materials. Custodial work is done by some sheltered workshops. Frequently, government service contracts supply the work for these workshops.

A sheltered workshop might be a good long-range work plan for some individuals. For others, a sheltered workshop can be a stepping-stone to supported employment.

According to the U.S. Department of Labor website, "supported employment provides assistance such as job coaches, transportation, assistive technology, specialized job training, and individually tailored supervision." The difference between a sheltered workshop and supported employment is the environment; supported employment happens in the community.

 Fact

According to the U.S. Department of Labor, there are four models of supported employment: individual placement model, enclave model (five to eight people placed at the same site), mobile work crew model (a small crew travels between locations, perhaps doing janitorial or groundskeeping work), and small business model (up to six people with disabilities work with a small group of nondisabled coworkers).

An individual might work in a restaurant, school, or company with the support of a job coach who will go to the site at key times and as needed. The individual also receives the *natural support* of those who work in that environment through their help, encouragement, and friendship. One of the benefits of supported employment is the social contact with others in the community.

CHAPTER 20

What Is the Goal?

By this time, you are not a stranger to goals. Even the most goal-oriented adult sees targeted outcomes with new determination when it involves a child with special needs. Goal setting may have started with an Individualized Family Service Plan in which your family outlined desired goals for your baby. As he enters school, an educational team will lead the way in developing needed academic, physical, and social goals for his IEP. As he prepares to leave high school, your child himself will lead the plan for his future.

Milestones for All Kids

Developmental milestones provide an estimate of the age when most children will develop a certain skill (sitting, smiling, saying a first word, talking, crawling, walking, or putting a simple puzzle together) and should not be taken as an absolute measure of a child's accomplishments. At the same time, developmental milestones are guidelines for child development and assist parents of a child with special needs in understanding what should be coming next. Developmental milestones are usually described in four categories: physical, social and emotional, communication, and cognitive.

Considerations for Children with Special Needs

In general, developmental milestones follow a sequence. Although a child with special needs may not be reaching the milestones at the same age as the baby next door, she is likely following the same *order* of development. Sometimes, however, a disability prevents the child from completing a milestone. Perhaps the milestone is skipped or perhaps it represents the stopping point of development in a particular area.

 Alert

> It is important to practice your child's goals on a regular basis. Your child is more likely to progress in making eye contact in conversation, for example, if it is consistently practiced. Encourage eye contact at the beginning of a conversation after school, at the dinner table, and at bedtime. You will see progress toward the goal.

A child with Down syndrome may seem to skip the stage of baby talk and begin talking by clearly pronouncing words in isolation. A child who is paralyzed from the waist down will obviously not continue past the sitting stage and attempt to stand. While she may have the arm strength to pull her body up, she will not have the leg strength or control to stand up.

Developmental Milestones

The "typical" order of physical milestones includes two areas: fine motor (done with the hands) and gross motor (involving the torso and limbs). The following is a sequence of *some* of the gross motor milestones. Note: The following milestones are provided by the Illinois Department of Human Services Early Intervention website.

Gross Motor Milestones

Sit with help	six months old
Crawl	nine months old
Pull to standing	twelve months old
Walk	fifteen months old
Walk up stairs	three years old

These are a few of the basic milestones; there are many additional ones. Again, these are guidelines for *the order of development* in most children.

Fine motor milestones are outlined below.

Fine Motor Milestones

Take hold of an object	four months
Move an object from one hand to the other	six months
Pick things up with the thumb and one finger	twelve months
Turn the pages of a book	two years

Professionals watch more than the movement of babies and toddlers to evaluate their development; they also watch social and emotional milestones. These are especially critical when it is suspected that a child is autistic.

Social and Emotional Milestones

Smile when someone speaks to her	three months
Give affection	twelve months
Begin to play with other children	four years

Communication milestones are critical when evaluating a child's hearing, cognitive skills, or her speech and language. Language skills are more than just saying the speech sounds correctly, and include understanding directions and being able to put words and sentences together to express ideas.

Communication Milestones	
Vocalize when someone speaks to her	four months
Say "mama" and "dada"	nine months
Say two or three words	twelve months
Use two or three words together	two years

It is easy to become frustrated when development seems to come easily for other children. A child with a special need may have to work much harder and longer to develop skills, while others pick them up spontaneously. Remember that the milestones do not represent small steps to your child. Rather, they are huge gaps that can require many small successes before they are fully accomplished.

Don't Compare Siblings

Comparing children within the same family (or even from different families) can create emotional upset. Children do not develop skills at the same ages, and every child is a unique person with strengths and weaknesses. (Read more about comparing siblings in Chapter 1.) This is especially true when one of the children has a disability. There are, however, some benefits of involving siblings in the goal process.

No one knows your child better than his siblings (and possibly yourself). His siblings share his child perspective on the world, family, neighborhood, and community. They undoubtedly have had many of the same experiences and will forever share memories from childhood. Siblings understand the pain that your child feels when he is teased by other children. They understand why he gets frustrated when things are difficult to do even though the same task may come easily to them.

Siblings can be the best encouragers for your child. He wants their approval and wants to be like them. He will work very hard at what they suggest, whether it is reaching for a toy, learning to tie his shoes, or studying the vocabulary for a science test.

 Fact

Children quickly stand up for a sibling with a special need. At home, they may demonstrate typical sibling rivalry and disagreements. But outside of the home, their reaction can be completely different. No one is allowed to pick on their family. Although you don't want your children fighting, standing up for a sibling is a quick way to affect family bonding.

Siblings (after a certain age) can offer valuable input on the "Now what?" question. The same way a sibling might suggest a logistic solution to a school problem (like leaving the afternoon books in a particular classroom because it is closer to the other afternoon classes than the locker is), she may have unique and valuable ideas about future goals. She knows her sibling well. She may be the one to suggest the perfect job or living arrangement.

The closeness of siblings has future benefits as well. A sibling is often the caregiver or trustee of a special-needs trust. At the very least (or most), a sibling is a confidant and advisor for life.

Family Goals

You may have written your child's Individualized Family Service Plan a few years ago, or it may still be a fresh, working document for your child's programming. Whichever is the case, thinking through the plan was probably the first time you really considered goals for your child's future. They were goals for the immediate future, involving how you wanted your child to communicate or function within your family structure. You planned things for your child to work on that you considered to be important.

Your child is a part of a family—your family. She will receive most of her guidance throughout her life from family members. Continue to develop goals that address your child as a part of your family long after the IFSP has ended. Here are some family involvement goals to consider:

- Routine family fun time
- Regular family discussions
- Opportunities for siblings to work together
- Involvement of sibling care
- One-on-one time with parents

How do these family goals impact the development of your child? They keep the family bond close. They teach siblings to look for each other during leisure time fun activities and as problem-solving buddies.

Character Education Goals

Character education is receiving a lot of attention in schools. You can focus on developing strong character in your child so he is prepared for life challenges.

Respect

Look for ways to teach your child respect. Naturally, that he shows respect to adults will be a personal family goal. It is important that he shows respect for others (his peers) as well as for himself. Self-esteem is a fragile thing, and unfortunately, your child will be in situations that can damage his self-concept. Build him up with lots of positives. If they are sincere, you will see a positive effect on how he sees himself. If the praise is less than sincere, he will interpret it as pity.

As his self-respect increases, showing respect for his peers will be easy. Even when they are less than encouraging, your child will be able to add a right-thinking boost to the situation. As he is respectful of them as individuals, they will be reminded to practice the same respect toward him.

Responsibility

Your child needs to be given responsibilities (see Chapter 8) to learn responsibility. He also needs to learn to be responsible for his actions. If the rule is that he straightens his room before the television goes on, stick to it. He should not be able to play up the fact that school was tough and he worked so hard all day. The rule is the rule. If your child learns responsibility with the little things, it will carry over to important tasks in life. Make teaching responsibility another one of your family goals.

Perseverance

A child with a disability works hard for his accomplishments in school and in therapy. It is tempting to give extra assistance to make up for all of the other challenges. Perhaps your child has a physical disability involving his hands. Making his bed in the morning can be a challenge for him, but given a little time he can do it. If he *can do it,* then let him! It is okay if he struggles a little to get the job done. In the long run, he will learn to stick with other, harder tasks as well.

Perseverance is perhaps one of the most important character traits to be learned. To keep on working toward the goal is a great way to approach life with a disability—never, ever give up.

Sometimes perseverance is the hardest one for parents to teach. Seeing a child work hard to accomplish little things can result in such compassion. Soon, things that the child could easily do are being done by the parent. After all, the child works so hard at everything. When she reaches the task that is the least bit confusing, she seeks help.

Sometimes, let her struggle. It is okay if she thinks that you are not sympathetic to her efforts. She will become a person who is confident in her problem solving ability.

Education Goals

As your child goes through the formal education years, there will be many goals. Most of them will be recorded on paper at the annual review meetings, but the goal-making process involves several steps before and after that meeting.

Be Aware of Peers

Always keep an eye on what your child's peers are doing. One of the best (and easiest) ways to do this is to volunteer at your child's school.

Seeing the books that are checked out of the library is a good indicator of the educational level of students. Although some kids select books that are too advanced for their reading level and some select books that are too simple, most will choose books that they can truly read for enjoyment.

If you need to better understand what the peers are doing socially, spend time at a park, movie theater, or pizza restaurant. You can easily observe social interactions, language, and styles.

Be Aware of State Benchmarks

You can read the learning standards and benchmarks for your state by going to the state board of education website. Your child's IEP will "be aligned to the state standards." That means that goals will be established in the subjects where your child shows a delay. The goals will address moving toward the desired benchmarks of learning for all students.

Be Aware of Your Child

As you become more familiar with your child's peers and the state's expectations for learners, consider your child's unique needs. You will need to think about the level of her current abilities. Remember that the small steps for some other children can be huge for your child.

Reaching the next level of educational or behavioral expectations probably won't "just happen." If that were the case, goals and therapies and IEP plans would not be needed. Work with your child's educational team to understand how to break down the goals into tiny, manageable steps. Make taking those steps a goal for your child and yourself.

Personal Goals

Keep sight of your child's personal goals. Although you may think that you know what your child would like to accomplish with his life, your perception may be different than what he is actually thinking.

Talk to Your Child

Talk to your child about *his* goals for the future. He may have aspirations of being a doctor. Perhaps he has the cognitive ability to pursue that dream. Start early to give him the experiences and educational opportunities to reach that goal. Many brilliant physicians have some type of special need that they have learned to manage.

If your child's abilities are not a realistic match for the goal of being a doctor, think about the many related medical professions. He may have chosen being a doctor because he has the most contact with a doctor in a medical setting. He wants to help people. There are many employees who help people in a hospital setting, including the receptionist at the information desk and the clerk in the gift shop.

Offer New Experiences

Continue to introduce your child to new experiences that build on his interests and abilities. Make it your goal—not your slave. Your child will be more likely to be interested in new experiences if neither of you is on overload. Remember that planning every minute of every day is the fast track to burnout, not the way to enrich lives.

Making a Plan

Have a plan for your child, yourself, and your family. The plan should include personal, educational, financial, and behavioral goals. It should include serious considerations and some breaks for fun.

The goals for your child (and how your family will support and encourage her efforts) should include short-term and long-term goals. Some of the short-term goals may even be recurring daily or weekly goals. Here are some examples:

- Sara will pick up her room after school.
- Sara will practice math facts with Dad for five minutes each evening.
- We will read one book together at bedtime.
- Sara will attend Brownies after school on Wednesdays.

Other goals will be more long-range. It is important to know where you are heading. Here are some long-range goals:

- Sara will maintain her room and show independent personal care with few reminders by age twelve.
- She will attempt to complete her homework assignments before she asks for help.
- Sara will gain one year of reading skills by the end of each school year.
- Sara will participate in one or two after-school activities when in high school.

A good goal set is always a mix of short-term and long-term items. A good goal set is also a balance of areas. Notice that Sara's goals include independence, academic skills, and activities with peers. The focus is not only on academics or only on socialization.

Checkups Along the Way

People change. Situations change. Goals should change as well. Periodically evaluate how everything is going. The key word here is *periodically.*

Progress (or lack of progress) toward a goal will happen over time. If your goal is for your child to keep his room picked up, you will monitor it on a daily basis. You will not, however, decide that he is not meeting that goal because one day his room is messy. At the end of the week or at the end of the month, look at the overall picture. Is he making progress toward keeping a neat room? Is it happening most of the time?

The other consideration with the periodic review of goals is that it should happen on a regular basis. Remember that it does not have to happen often, but it does have to happen on some kind of a schedule.

As you evaluate goal progress, make needed adjustments. Perhaps the goal involves saving for your child's special-needs trust. If you or your spouse has gotten a significant raise since you set up your savings plan, the periodic checkup will help you remember to increase the amount you are saving toward that goal.

Create goals for your child, your family, and yourself. Review them periodically. Make adjustments as needed.

CHAPTER 21

Advocacy

It is natural for parents to want what is best for their children. However, those "best things" don't always come along spontaneously. Sometimes the things a child needs must be defined and requested. Often the advocacy process is simply the everyday interaction with people in your child's life, and sometimes it is more formal. Encourage those who are close to your child (as well as your child herself) to become fair, yet confident, advocates.

What Is an Advocate?

An *advocate* is defined as "one that pleads the cause of another" by the *Merriam-Webster's Collegiate Dictionary*. As soon as you were aware that your child had a special need you naturally became his advocate. Other people throughout his childhood and teen years will also plead the cause of his needs. By the time he is an adult, he will have learned the valuable skill of self-advocacy.

Advocacy in Your Family

After you address important medical decisions regarding your baby's care as a newborn, you will be ready to turn to advocacy in other areas of his life. Talking to your family will be the first task.

Perhaps you and your family had forewarning about your baby's needs. Often, though, a complication at birth or some unknown factor made it a surprise. You did not realize that your baby would have special needs.

It is important to be honest and yet sensitive as you initially talk with your family. If you are talking to your other children, they probably do not need too many details. "Joey has a special machine that will help him breathe. We have to be careful not to touch the tubes on the machine."

 Fact

> Your extended family (your baby's grandparents, aunts, and uncles) may benefit from attending an information presentation or from observing a program that serves infants with special needs. They will be able to ask questions that they may be reluctant to ask you. They will also see how other babies are overcoming their special needs.

Your own parents are probably well aware of the medical struggles of your baby. But if the disability is not discovered until the school years, it could be a different story. Suppose you find out that your child has a cognitive delay and will be in special education classes. It is important to present your child's needs honestly with the amount of information that your family is ready to hear. You can further explain details as time goes on and they have become more adjusted to the news. Your child is still their cherished grandchild, and you are doing everything in your power to make the right choices for him.

Advocacy with Your Child's Peers

Your child may not be ready for a preschool play group at the community center when he is three, but sooner or later he will be in groups with other children. Children are accepting, supportive, and yet sometimes unknowingly cruel.

When your child first begins to take part in social groups, take part as well. Are the children blowing bubbles at a park? Give your child some chances to blow bubbles. Since this might be hard, offer to take some turns blowing so that everyone can catch the bubbles. The peers will see different ways that your child can play. They will become more open to including him in their fun.

 Essential

Always be on the lookout for ways to include your child in the activities of other children. He doesn't have to do everything they do. He may not be interested in many activities. That is his prerogative as a person. However, when he is interested, be quick to make on-the-spot adjustments so the activity will work for him, too.

Advocacy in Your Community

You may live in a large city where awareness of disabilities is strong, or you may live in a rural area where your child is the only one with a special need. Take a look at the community activities of yourself and your family and be proactive by talking about ways your child can participate. Give lots of positive feedback to those who make the effort to be helpful.

Become a coach for a community ball league in which your child would like to participate. The other coaches and the children on the team will get to know you and your child as people. The special need will be secondary. As you work with all the children, you will be an advocate for your child's unique needs. Soon some of the children will take over the role of advocate.

Advocacy at School

Be involved at school. Let your child's teacher and administration know that you want to do everything you can to help, but that you will not be a meddler. Volunteer where the school needs help, and you will see a natural, positive response to the needs of your child. Why? You are not telling them how to do their jobs. Instead, you are offering to be a team player.

Sometimes you will want to volunteer to make an activity more accessible to your child. For example, perhaps there is an after-school carnival run by the PTO. Your child would like to participate in the ball pit, but a physical disability makes it difficult. He is able to do all of the other activities independently. Sign up to help in the ball pit. You will be a part of the overall activity, and you will be an advocate for your child.

Sometimes you will need to be an advocate for your child to have services that you feel are appropriate. Bring examples of your child's class work that represent areas of your concern. During a discussion with your child's teacher or in a formal IEP meeting, you are your child's best advocate when you stay calm.

Who Can Be an Advocate?

Anyone who is helpful in promoting your child's well-being by pleading her cause is an advocate.

There are several considerations regarding who might be a truly helpful advocate:

- The person must be knowledgeable of the condition or special need.
- The person should be knowledgeable about how the condition impacts your child.
- The person should be tactful, using fact and not emotion in his appeal.
- The person should be able to offer constructive ideas to address the concern.

It can be a family member or friend, special education professional, medical professional, lawyer, parent of a child with a special need, or a person who is himself disabled.

Everyday Tips

You have been an advocate for your child since the day he was
born. Looking out for his needs, asking questions, requesting information and services—you have voiced his needs and rights on his
behalf. Developing everyday advocacy techniques that are effective and not alienating is your goal.

Rewording

Sometimes you will field comments or questions that are offensive. You have two choices:

- You can inform the speaker that his words were offensive.
- You can reword his comment or question in more appropriate language before you give your response.

Most of the time offensive errors will be unintentional. Perhaps
you and your child are waiting for a ride at a theme park. When it
is your turn to climb onboard the attendant remarks that she didn't
know that he was a crippled boy. You cringe. He is a little boy with
a physical disability. You might say he has a special need. You
would not use the label *crippled* and you certainly would not use
the label in front of the child.

Sometimes, there are other reasons for unintentional offense.
An example is the media—newspapers and Internet. Too often
the space allowed for titles dictates word order. It is not intended
to offend. In those instances, read further to see how the article is
written.

Be Proactive

Communicate the positive ideas and strategies that you want to be associated with your child. This will be critical amongst your family and friends, at school, and in the community. You may feel like you are saying the same thing over and over. It takes a long time to mold thinking and words.

 Essential

Try to build up understanding of your child's unique needs before there is a problem. If the other person or organization understands your child as a person, and sees how she can be successful with the necessary accommodations, they will be more open to your requests.

Perhaps your child is involved in a community youth group. The group will have a car wash fundraiser. Your child may use crutches to walk because spina bifida affects the use of his legs.

At the parent planning meeting the idea of the car wash is presented. Your response is positive. "That's a great idea. David is a wonderful artist. I am sure that he would love to help with the posters." You have reminded the group about the *ability* of your child and that he can be involved despite his disability.

Pick Your Battles

You will not be able to change the world. You can only promote, encourage, and reword so much on behalf of your child. Make sure that your battles are for the things that are truly important. Here are some examples:

- Your child is in physical danger.

- The offense continues to happen over time despite your polite efforts for change.
- The offense is committed by a person in leadership who will likely influence others to follow his practice.
- The offense goes against your child's legal rights.

In these instances, though, you will need to confront the offender. These situations will hopefully be few in number.

Join a Group

Get involved in a group that promotes awareness of your child's particular need. Typically, there are national groups for most disabilities, and many have sub-groups at the state (and sometimes community) level. Being involved in an awareness group can mean anything from attending informational workshops and conferences to lobbying for needed legislation. You will be able to find activities within the group that fit your personality. Perhaps the most important aspect of your involvement is showing your child that he is important, and that it is important to communicate his needs to his world.

Using an Advocate

Sometimes the thought of using an advocate can be scary. You might feel that you are confronting the person you're asking to be an advocate. Or, the people the advocate will be addressing may feel threatened. The role of an advocate is not to attack but to *plead the cause* as the definition states.

For Information

Perhaps your child has a low-incidence medical condition that will impact her ability to do her schoolwork. You want the school nurse, principal, and teachers to have a clear understanding of what to expect from and what to require of your child. An advocate might come in to present information on your child's condition, offer guidelines for how modify her school program, and answer questions.

 Fact

Sometimes you can use a DVD or pamphlets for advocacy. The information in such material is presented in a straightforward, factual way that can be applied to the needs of your child without being confrontational. A bulleted list of facts about the condition can also be helpful.

To Explain Things Differently

Perhaps you have explained your child's needs to her community dance teacher. You believe that she can do well in the class with a few accommodations, but the teacher does not seem to understand your child's needs or your requests as a parent. An advocate might be able to explain the same things differently and more effectively.

As Another Set of Ears

Sometimes you will be seeking another set of ears—for yourself and your spouse. You believe that your request for adaptive swimming lessons at the community pool is fair. You have explained the number of children it will serve. Perhaps you are not understanding the concerns of the recreation board. An advocate could help you understand what they are trying to communicate, and facilitate the discussion.

When You Are Frustrated

In whatever situation you are advocating for your child, you can become frustrated. You are hoping to secure something for your child, who is, of course, near to your heart. When emotion gets in the way of your efforts, an advocate can help. Having an advocate doesn't always mean that you will succeed in getting what you want, but the advocate can interact in a calm, less emotional manner.

Advocacy Groups

Conducting a computer search for advocacy groups is a good starting point for finding a group in your area. You can also get information by searching the website of national organizations. Advocates from these organizations are active in several ways.

Advocates and Schools

An advocate might attend a school meeting with parents. The advocate may suggest ideas for things that will address the child's needs, ask questions in addition to those asked by the family, or simply listen and take notes for the parents to review later.

 Essential

Try to inform the other professionals attending the meeting that you will be bringing an advocate. It is only common courtesy, and will dispel the idea that you are trying to spring a surprise on them. If possible, tell them about the advocate at the time the meeting is set up.

Parents who have attended IEP or 504 meetings will vouch for the difficulty of remembering everything discussed. Even with copies of the forms and reports, it is hard to remember the helpful and important details of discussions.

Advocates as Presenters

Sometimes advocates will speak about a particular disability or condition to a school or community group. It might be made to parents or siblings of children with the condition. Some advocates distribute literature from a booth at a fair or festival.

Teaching Self-Advocacy

The ultimate goal of advocacy is for the child to learn to request needed services. This is a long, gradual process, but it should begin at an early age. At some point in time, the child will become an adult and will be fending for her own rights and needs in the community.

Language of Self-Advocacy

The language of self-advocacy is related to needs and wants. First of all, your child will learn which things she would like to have (wants) and which things she needs and often has a legal right to have. "Please" and "thank you" are important add-ons to advocacy language. A child with beginning language skills might simply start with "Help, please."

 Fact

Your child's IEP or 504 plan will outline the modifications and accommodations of her school program. She has a legal right to them. However, things do not always happen smoothly just because they are written down. Reminding a teacher politely is always great self-advocacy. Chances are there has been an oversight or misunderstanding of what is needed.

Here are some examples of self-advocacy language for a child with a learning disability.

- "I tried to read these instructions, but I am stuck. Would you please read them for me?"

- "Please read that test question again."
- "I am supposed to go to Mrs. Smith's room to take my test. May I go there now?"
- "May I get a multiplication chart for this assignment, please?"

A high-school-aged child might politely talk about the modifications and accommodations on her IEP. A college student might request reader services through a designated office of support services.

Advocacy Attempts

Encourage your child to start being her own advocate as soon as she has mastered some of the language. (A preschooler might be able to ask for help unzipping her book bag.) Sometimes she might ask for something that is one of her IEP goals. Maybe the physical therapist is working with her on zipping things. Your child may not get help with the backpack zipper when she asks because school staff members are working with her in that area.

Sometimes children ask for things that are not advocacy requests. An example is the child who is deaf asking her interpreter to go to her locker between classes. Does she have special needs? Sure, but her communication needs do not prevent her from going to her locker.

Sometimes your child might make a perfectly legitimate request in a polite manner, only to be refused. Perhaps your teen requests that a test be read (and that is listed on her IEP), but she is told to read it on her own. Be her advocate and talk with the teacher about your teen's IEP.

Rest assured that your child's school is not out to work against you or to deny your child her rights. Calm discussion as your child's advocate will address most, if not all, of your concerns.

CHAPTER 22

Plan for the Future

E very parent's goal is for their children to be happily settled in their adult life. While parents cherish the joys and memories of their children growing up, the focus is always on preparing them for the future. Preparing the child with special needs requires additional focus and considerations. There are many choices and plans to be made before "happily settling into adulthood."

Emotional Preparation

A child with special needs will go through the same emotional stages as other children—and then some! At some point a baby will go through separation anxiety whether or not the baby has a special need. She will do things for attention as a toddler and young child. Years later, the same "child" will show some form of rebellion (although it may appear to be minimal) as she enters adulthood.

Family Bonds

A strong family bond gives the child a stabilizing influence and something to fall back on when things are difficult. If there is a strong bond across the family, siblings are more likely to seek each other's support as adults during periods of trauma and stress. They are also more likely to trust others (such as spouses) for the same emotional support because they had healthy family bonding as children.

Asking for Help

Healthy emotional preparation for life also involves the ability to ask for help. Everyone needs help sometimes. It is important for your child to know when and how to ask for help and when it is a situation she should be trying on her own.

A good indicator of a child's ability to understand how and when to ask for help is how she approaches her homework. Perhaps she is completing a worksheet on the day's social studies lesson. She easily finds the answers for the first three questions, but the fourth question is not as easy. Hopefully, she will skip the difficult question and complete the rest of the page. She may even find the tricky answer as she is doing so. If not, she will go back to the question after she has completed the rest of the sheet and look for that answer again. If she still has difficulty, then she will ask for help. She will ask—that is important. It is equally important that she tried (in several ways) before asking.

Independence

In the worksheet example above, the child demonstrated independence. Her goal was to complete the activity as best she could. Her goal was not to expect help before trying. Independence in life is important. Adulthood seldom includes someone to jump in and give the answer.

Extended Family

Your child's relationship with extended family members will also contribute to her emotional preparation for life. Through these relationships she will exercise communication and social skills outside of her immediate family.

In most situations, extended family will encourage the child to practice communication, social skills, and independence. On occasion, parents will need to remind extended family members not to coddle or talk down to the child. In other instances, the expectations may be unrealistic for the child. For example, the child who is autistic will have difficulty with change in routine. Expecting her to be excited when Grandma comes to stay in her room is unrealistic. She may love Grandma dearly, but the change in routine will be unsettling to her. This is a chance to teach the family about the unique needs of your child. Make sure that your child has lots of opportunities to interact with extended family.

Experiences with Non–Family Members

Interacting with non–family members can help your child prepare for the future as well. Contact with non–family members such as teachers, coaches, child care providers, club sponsors, friends, and neighbors can give your child opportunities to practice the same communication and social skills. In most situations, she will be challenged to be more independent. Although others may be anxious to help (sometimes too much), it can take a while for them to decide *how* to help. Very often a child will go ahead and do for herself.

Interaction Outside the Home

People do not live in isolation. Children who are neglected in orphanages do not thrive. Adults who are separated from loved ones become lonely, craving conversation and companionship. The same is true for the adult with special needs. It is important to have contact and support from family members. It is also important to be involved with groups created to meet the needs of those with special needs.

Organizations for Adults with Special Needs

Organizations for adults with special needs fall into several categories: social organizations, service organizations, and advocacy groups. In some instances, a group might serve more than one purpose.

Social organizations may be focused on individuals with a particular need and those individuals who work with them or are relatives. Often these groups are also service organizations. In some situations, there are separate service organizations for professionals. Most of the organizations have an advocacy segment. See Chapter 21 for more information.

Some examples of disability related groups are:

- The Arc (previously the Association for Retarded Citizens of the United States)
- The American Foundation for the Blind
- The Learning Disabilities Association of America
- The National Association of the Deaf
- United Cerebral Palsy Association
- Children and Adults with Attention Deficit/Hyperactivity Disorder
- The Epilepsy Foundation

In addition to national or statewide organizations, many smaller local groups also exist.

A local group might have a service purpose. Message relay services for the deaf, for example, were operated in separate locations independently before such services became law. Socialization might also be the purpose of another group, such as a social club of college students with learning disabilities.

Family Support

Developing family support for the future begins with family traditions (Chapter 9) and teaching responsibility within a family (Chapter 8). All children in the family learn the importance of a strong family support system. They learn responsibilities to help the household run smoothly and a commitment to address needs within the family. These instilled values and responsibilities carry over into adulthood.

Living Arrangements

Adult siblings may share living accommodations, but siblings do not have to live together to provide family support in this area. Siblings may coordinate or monitor other arrangements for the sibling with special needs, such as a group home in the community. Siblings may hire a part- or full-time independent care aide to assist the sibling with a disability in her own apartment or house.

Emotional Support

Even if adult siblings are separated geographically, cell phones and computers allow them to keep in touch with minimal cost. Pay-as-you-go-type cell phones are reasonably priced alternatives to a lengthy cell phone plan. For some adults with disabilities, the pay-as-you-go phones are a quick solution to communication and safety needs. And purchasing a computer is not necessary to keep in touch by e-mail. Computers are often available for use in group homes as well as in public libraries.

Financial Support

In some families, there is an understood financial responsibility between siblings. In the case of an adult sibling with a disability, another sibling might help out with basic living expenses (food, rent, and clothing). Or, perhaps the basic expenses are covered by SSI or a job. Then the sibling might help with some of the "extras" like an occasional night out to eat, movie rental, or inclusion on a family vacation. The overall financial resources of the adult with special needs might include wages from employment, SSI, Supplement Payment Program funds, a special-needs trust, and some money from an adult sibling.

Day-to-Day Business

Siblings can offer support in the area of day-to-day business as well. Making appointments, assisting in paying bills, arranging transportation, purchasing clothing and food, and entertainment outings are areas where the siblings may help complete the task or actually help financially.

Living Arrangements

Planning for the future must involve consideration of living arrangements. Even if your adult child is living at home, the time will come when you will be unable to care for him. Planning for those arrangements now does not mean they have to happen now. It is a good idea, though, to make sure he has lots of experiences staying elsewhere so that living outside your home will not be completely foreign to him.

Living with a Family Member

Some families continue to care for a disabled family member after the death (or inability to provide care) of the individual's parents. In this situation, it is sometimes an adult sibling who assumes the caregiver's role.

Certain states have provision for some financial reimbursement for those providing a private home environment for the individual with a disability. This arrangement (and funding) is also available for a non–family member who is providing a home.

Other Living Arrangements

If the individual does not live independently and does not live with a family member, he may live in a subsidized private housing arrangement, a group home, or an institution. Chapter 17 explains alternate living arrangements in more detail.

Income

Everyone needs money to live. It is true of the individual with a disability who lives independently in the community, as well as those who live in a group home or even an institution. Every person shares the same basic human needs of food and shelter. Many individuals with disabilities are self-supporting as adults. Others are unable to support themselves financially or may be able to only partially meet their financial needs.

Employment

Perhaps your adult child will be gainfully employed in a job that supports her living expenses. She may work at the local mall or may be a licensed hairstylist. She may have her doctorate and teach at a university. Additional information about attaining education and career goals is found in Chapters 18 and 19.

While a U.S. Census report (May 2008) states that 56 percent of people with a disability were employed last year, the median income of those individuals with a *nonsevere disability* was $22,000. The median income for individuals who are severely disabled was $12,800.

The range of income and financial needs of every person varies greatly. Needs are dependent on living arrangements, life style, and medical expenses. If your adult child is unable to meet her financial needs through employment, she may be eligible for a government program to help her meet those needs and obligations.

Government Programs

Social Security Insurance (SSI) and Social Security Disability Insurance (SSDI) are programs that provide monthly income to qualified individuals. Assets and disability are two of the considerations. See Chapters 6 and 19 for more information.

Adults with a disability may also qualify for additional funding through their state-operated Supplemental Payment Program. Receiving money from this program is not dependent on receiving SSI. However, certain living arrangements are required, such as a group home, foster care home, a community home for individuals with disability, or a transitional living arrangement. The purpose of the Supplemental Payment Program is to assist individuals with a disability to maintain a basic standard of living. For additional information on your state's program and how to apply, search for "Supplemental Payment Program" plus the name of your state. In some states, an application is not necessary, as monetary awards are made based on the disability information on file with the state through the SSI program.

Income or financial support may also come from arrangements set up by parents and other family members. The options and arrangements should be considered carefully.

Other Finances

As the parent of a child with a special need, you will be assisting him in planning to ensure that his financial future is stable. If your child has proven that he is able to complete a formal postsecondary education program and pay his bills through gainful employment, you may consider leaving him an inheritance through a will. If he is unable to handle finances, you may wish to consider a special-needs trust.

Trusts and Wills

Consider ways that your financial resources can meet the needs of your child throughout his adult life. If you choose to leave money to your child through a will, there may be some drawbacks.

- Even a very small amount of money in assets can disqualify an individual from receiving government funding.
- Money inherited through a will must be managed. Who will assist your adult child in managing his money?
- Money inherited from a will is a set amount. When that money is exhausted it is gone. Who will provide financial

support for your adult child when the finances from the will have been depleted?

Leaving funds to your adult child through a will that lacks special provisions basically says: "Here is the money. It is your job to make it work." Many adult children with disabilities are unable to handle basic monthly financial obligations much less the responsibility of large-sum money management over a lifetime.

Special-Needs Trusts

A special-needs trust (sometimes called a "supplemental needs trust") also requires a legal document. It outlines specifically how money is to be used. It designates an individual as a trustee to oversee the use of the money and to manage how the funds will be invested. Write the special-needs trust carefully so that it does not take away from any government funding your child may receive. Unless you are very, very wealthy, your adult child will need both kinds of "income" to maintain his living expenses and some basic "wants."

 Fact

Shop around for financial services to establish your child's special-needs trust. Some offices will charge a fee as well as taking additional commissions. Others, such as the National Association of Personal Advisors, will only charge a fee.

Parents can calculate the estimated costs of living for their child at the Merrill Lynch website. After entering basic information (age, disability, known financial needs for medications and equipment), the calculator can give parents an idea of what they should consider as their child's financial needs for the future. The Merrill Lynch site also has information on financial planning for children with specific special needs, including hearing loss, vision impairment, and autism.

Insurance Costs

The medical expenses of a special need do not disappear when the child becomes an adult. The initial costs incurred when the child's disability was discovered (initial evaluations, corrective surgeries, and therapies) *may* lessen with time.

An aging body seems to undo some childhood surgeries. The typical effects of aging can also impact the child's illness or condition. It is crucial that your adult child have adequate health insurance over her lifetime.

Private Health Insurance

If your adult child is working, she may have health insurance through her place of employment. She may be eligible to remain on your health insurance as a dependent disabled adult. Medicaid, a government insurance program for low-income families and individuals, may be another option.

Adults with a disability may qualify for additional government-sponsored medical care programs (separate from Medicaid). Among other things, the severity of the disability and the income of the applicant will be reviewed. The recipient may be responsible for the initial cost of some medical expenses. Search "medical insurance disabled adult" and the name of your state.

Health insurance is a critical, ongoing need for the adult with special needs. Insurance services and options can be confusing, but it is important to understand your child's choices and to assist her in getting a health care program to meet her needs.

Bibliography and Websites for Parents of Children with Special Needs

Resources for All Ages

Attention Deficit and Learning Disability

Children and Adults with Attention Deficit/Hyperactivity Disorder
This site provides resources for educators, parents, and members of the community.
www.chadd.org

Learning Disabilities Association of America
This site has information about three types of learning disabilities and related disorders.
www.ldanatl.org

Autism

National Institute of Neurological Disorders and Stroke
This site has information on autism.
www.ninds.nih.gov/disorders/autism/detail_autism.htm

Pyramid Educational Consultants
This is the official site of the Picture Exchange Communication System (PECS).
www.pecs.com

Developmental Delay

The ArcLink.org
The site of this national organization for the mentally retarded provides information for families and community leaders.
www.thearclink.org/links/index.asp

National Association for Down Syndrome
This site has information resources for parents and caregivers regarding Down syndrome.
www.nads.org/index.html

Education

ED.gov—U.S. Department of Education
This site has information about educating a child with special needs.
www.ed.gov/parents/needs/speced/edpicks.jhtml?src=ln

Financial

Lawyers.com
This site explains legalities and important considerations in forming a special-needs trust.
http://trusts-estates.lawyers.com/estate-planning/Special-Needs-Trusts.html

Merrill Lynch
This site is a resource for calculating and planning the lifelong financial needs of a child with special needs.
www.totalmerrill.com/TotalMerrill/pages /ArticleViewer.aspx?TITLE=specialneedstrusts

The National Association of Personal Financial Advisors
This site has information on establishing a special-needs trust.
www.napfa.org

Social Security Online— Supplemental Security Income (SSI)
This site provides information on eligibility for Social Security Income.
www.ssa.gov/ssi

USAToday.com
This article addresses considerations in planning a special-needs trust.
www.usatoday.com/money/perfi /columnist/block/0025.htm

General Information

ARCH National Respite Network
This site contains information about respite care services and programs.
http://chtop.org/ARCH.html

Centers for Disease Control and Prevention
This site has information about the prevention and treatment of diseases and conditions affecting children with special needs.
www.cdc.gov/index.htm

Cornucopia of Disability Information
This site lists Internet resources for many areas of disability.
http://codi.buffalo.edu

The Council for Exceptional Children
This is the official site of the Council for Exceptional Children. It has information for teachers and parents about children with exceptional needs.
www.cec.sped.org/AM/Template.cfm? Section=About_CEC

The Disability Resources Monthly Regional Resources Directory
This is a listing of disability related agencies and organizations categorized by state.
www.disabilityresources.org/DRMreg.html

Disabled World
This site gives information on famous people with disabilities.
www.disabled-world.com/artman /publish/article_0060.shtml

Easter Seals Disability Services
This site describes various disabilities as well as therapy services.
www.easterseals.com/site/PageServer

***Eunice Kennedy Shriver* National Institute of Child Health and Human Development**
This site supports research of various types of disabilities.
www.nichd.nih.gov

Illinois Department of Human Services: Early Intervention—Milestones of Developmental Growth
This site lists basic developmental skills according to age, from one month to five years.
www.state.il.us/agency/dhs/earlyint /ei02parentlwicd.html

Make-a-Wish Foundation
This site provides information about granting wishes for children with life-threatening illnesses.
www.wish.org/about

National Dissemination Center for Children with Disabilities
This site has a listing of State Resource Sheets of agencies that serve children with disabilities.
www.nichcy.org/states.htm

National Rehabilitation Information Center
This site links to a collection of resources (including agencies and reports) related to disabilities.
www.naric.com

NICHCY—Children's Literature and Disability
This site contains a list of books for children about various disabilities.
www.nichcy.org/FamiliesAndCommunity /Pages/Default.aspx

U.S. Census Bureau
This site gives disability data by type and age.
www.census.gov/hhes/www /disability/disability.html

Hearing Loss

Lions Club International
This site describes an organization with programs for children who are deaf or blind.
www.lionsclubs.org/EN/content /about_index.shtml

National Association of the Deaf
This site lists information about the organization as well as links to Affiliate Members: Advocacy/Social Organizations, ASL/Interpreter Training Programs, Captioning Agencies, Colleges/Universities, Commissions on the Deaf and Hard of Hearing, Schools for the Deaf, and more.
www.nad.org/site/pp.asp?c=foINKQMBF&b =764837

Legal

Americans with Disabilities Act
This site contains information about the Americans with Disabilities Act as it pertains to employment, education, and community considerations.
www.ada.gov

Federal Communications Commission —Disability Rights Office
This site explains the laws governing telecommunications rights of those with a hearing, vision, or speech disability.
www.fcc.gov/cgb/dro

FedLaw—Disabilities
This is a list of links to federal laws pertaining to disabilities.
www.thecre.com/fedlaw/legal6a.htm

Medical

American Academy of Pediatrics

This site contains an online referral service for finding a pediatrician.

https://www.nfaap.org/netforum/eweb /dynamicpage.aspx?site=nf.aap .org&webcode=aapmbr_prsSearch &CFID=5460234&CFTOKEN=45500073

American College of Rheumatology

This site offers information about arthritis in children.

www.rheumatology.org/public/factsheets /diseases_and_conditions/juvenilearthritis .asp

Centers for Medicare and Medicaid Services

This site defines the services and eligibility determinations for Medicaid and the State Children's Health Insurance Program.

www.cms.hhs.gov/home/medicaid.asp

Cystic Fibrosis Foundation

This site provides information about cause, treatment, and research associated with cystic fibrosis.

www.cff.org/AboutCF

Emergency Medical Form for Children with Special Needs

This is an online form that can be printed and kept for emergencies. It was created by the American College of Emergency Physicians and the American Academy of Pediatrics.

www.aap.org/advocacy/blankform.pdf

Epilepsy Foundation

This site offers medical facts and practical ideas for living with epilepsy.

www.epilepsyfoundation.org

Muscular Dystrophy Association

This site has information about the MDA services and the Jerry Lewis Telethon.

www.mda.org

The National Association for Albinism and Hypopigmentation

This site has information on the causes and treatments for albinism.

www.albinism.org/publications/what_is _albinism.html

National Association of Children's Hospitals and Related Institutions

This site has information on finding children's hospitals and services nationwide.

www.childrenshospitals.net/AM/Template .cfm?Section=Hospital_Profile_Search &Template=/CustomSource/Hospital Profiles/HospitalProfileSearch.cfm

National Newborn Screening Status Report—American Pregnancy Association

This online document lists the newborn screening required by state.

www.americanpregnancy.org/labornbirth /newborntesting.htm

Ronald McDonald House Charities

This site has information about Ronald McDonald houses and Ronald McDonald rooms for families of children who are hospitalized.

www.rmhc.com

SAMHSA's National Mental Health Information Center

This site reports on learning disabilities, autism, and behavior disorders.

http://mentalhealth.samhsa.gov /publications/allpubs/CA-0006/default.asp

Shriners Hospitals for Children

The site lists the locations of twenty-two free hospitals for children.

www.shrinershq.org/Hospitals/Main

St. Jude Children's Research Hospital

The hospital site describes available care for children with cancer or other serious illness.

www.stjude.org/about

U.S. Department of Health and Human Services—Insure Kids Now!

Read about low or no cost insurance options for children.

www.insurekidsnow.gov

Speech and Language

American Speech-Language-Hearing Association

This site has information about speech and language services.

www.asha.org/default.htm

Sports and Recreation

American Academy of Physical Medicine and Rehabilitation

This site has a directory of organizations for athletes who have a disability.

www.aapmr.org/condtreat/athletes.htm

Disability Travel and Recreation Resources

This site provides links to travel and recreation information.

www.makoa.org/travel.htm

National Ability Center

This site has information on sports and recreation programs and camps for individuals with special needs.

www.discovernac.org/index.htm

National Sports Center for the Disabled

This site has links to sports-related topics for individuals who are disabled.

www.nscd.org

Special Olympics

This site has information about the recreational and competitive events of the Special Olympics.

www.specialolympics.org/Special +Olympics+Public+Website/English /About_Us/default.htm

Visual Impairment

American Foundation for the Blind

This site has information about blindness and available services.

www.afb.org/default.asp

American Printing House for the Blind

This site has information about braille materials, computer software, and other products of help to individuals who are blind.

www.aph.org

The Braille Institute

This site has information about services and products for those who are blind. It includes information about Braille publishing and recorded media.

www.brailleinstitute.org

Lions Club International

This site describes an organization with programs for children who are deaf or blind.

www.lionsclubs.org/EN/php/index.shtml

National Federation of the Blind

This site is a resource of information and services for individuals who are blind.

www.nfb.org/nfb/About_the_NFB.asp? SnID=1452631885

National Organization of Parents of Blind Children

This site provides information and support for parents of children who are blind.

www.nfb.org/nfb/NOPBC_About_Us.asp

Postsecondary and Adult Child Information

Driver Education

The Association for Driving Rehabilitation Specialists

This site has information about driver education and training for persons with disabilities as well as assessment considerations for individuals with various disabilities.

www.driver-ed.org/i4a/pages/index.cfm?pageid=1

Model Practices for Driver Rehabilitation for Individuals with Disabilities

This document has resources for driver rehabilitation and information on equipment dealers.

www.aded.net/files/public/Model_Practices_Final2.pdf

Employment

Bureau of Labor Statistics

This site has the Consumer Price Index Summary.

www.bls.gov/news.release/cpi.nr0.htm

Employment and Disability Guide, Cornell University

This is an online guide to questions, concerns, and laws pertaining to individuals with disabilities in the work place.

www.ilr.cornell.edu/library/research/subject Guides/employmentAndDisability.html

Job Accommodation Network

This is a government site that provides information on resources for workers with disabilities.

http://janweb.icdi.wvu.edu/links/adalinks.htm

Job Seeking Skills for People with Disabilities (Cal State University —Northridge)

This site provides information for setting career goals and looking for work.

www.csun.edu/~sp20558/dis/acknowledgements.html

Succeeding Together: People with Disabilities in the Workforce (Cal State University—Northridge)

This site gives tips to employers and employees on successful work strategies.

www.csun.edu/~sp20558/dis/emcontents.html

U.S. Department of Labor— Supported Employment

This site describes the supported employment model of work.

www.dol.gov/odep/archives/fact/supportd.htm

U.S. Department of Labor—Transition Programs and Services

This site has information on school-to-work transition services.

www.dol.gov/odep/documents/transition_programs.htm

Vocational Rehabilitation (Rehabilitation Services Administration)

This site has ways to contact VR for career counseling and education funding for qualified students.
www.ed.gov/about/offices/list/osers/rsa/about.html

Living Arrangements

MR/DD Living

This site has information for residential services options for adults who are mentally retarded.
www.mrddliving.com

Medical

The Med-Cal Program

This site describes the application process for health services for adults with a disability in the state of California.
www.medi-cal.ca.gov

Postsecondary Education

The ACT

This site provides information for students with disabilities wishing to request testing accommodations.
www.act.org/aap/disab/index.html

College Board Accuplacer Test

This site provides information on how academic skills of students are assessed. Students may request accommodations.
www.collegeboard.com/student/testing/accuplacer

College Board Testing—Services for Students with Disabilities

This site includes information on requesting accommodations for tests offered by the College Board.
www.collegeboard.com/ssd/student/index.html

College Funding for Students with Disabilities

This site explains a number of ways to fund college.
www.washington.edu/doit/Brochures/Academics/financial-aid.html

FinAid!

This site explains how to search for scholarships. Some are specifically for students with special needs.
www.finaid.org/otheraid/disabled.phtml

HEATH Resource Center

This site has financial aid information for students with disabilities.
www.heath.gwu.edu

National Federation of the Blind Scholarship Program

This program offers annual scholarships to students who are blind.
www.nfb.org/nfb/scholarship_program.asp?SnID=1094328070

PEPNet

A resource of information for deaf and hard of hearing individuals who wish to pursue postsecondary education.
www.pepnet.org/default.asp

PSAT/NMSQT

Read information on how to request accommodations for the PSAT test.
www.collegeboard.com/student/testing/psat/about.html

The SAT
Accommodation information for the SAT
is available on this site.
www.collegeboard.com/ssd/student/
index.html

Autism Books

McClannahan, Lynn and Krantz, Patricia.
Activity Schedules for Children With
Autism: Teaching Independent Behavior.
(Bethesda, MD: Woodbine House, 1999).
Mesibov, Gary, Shea, Victoria, and
Schopler, Eric. *The TEACCH Approach to*
Autism Spectrum Disorders. (New York:
Springer, 2004).

Glossary

ADHD coach: A professional who works with individuals with ADHD to set goals, utilize strategies, and evaluate progress in managing their disability.

Albinism: A genetic birth defect that is manifested in the child having little or no pigmentation in his skin or eyes as well as vision problems.

Amniocentesis: A prenatal test for genetic and chromosomal birth defects that is done by removing a small amount of amniotic fluid.

Amplification: A hearing aid, FM auditory trainer, or cochlear implant.

Anencephaly: A neural tube defect in which the brain does not form.

Annual review: The meeting held once a year to look at a child's progress on IEP goals and to create a new IEP for the upcoming year.

Anxiety disorder: An emotional disorder of extreme stress in everyday situations.

Asperger syndrome: An autism spectrum disorder that impacts communication and social skills. A child with Asperger syndrome is typically considered to have normal intelligence.

Assistive device: Any equipment used to perform a daily task, such as a cane or walker.

Assistive technology: Technology used for communication (such as a communication board) or to manage a disability (such as an electronic speller used to manage a learning disability).

Astigmatism: The condition of an irregularly shaped lens or cornea (often incorrectly called "stigmatism").

Attention deficit disorder (ADD): A condition manifested by the inability to maintain focus on everyday tasks, particularly listening to a speaker or completing a chore or a classroom assignment.

Attention deficit/hyperactivity disorder (ADHD): A condition manifested by the inability to maintain focus and excessive movement (inability to sit still).

Audiologist: A professional who tests hearing acuity and auditory processing.

Autism: A disorder involving difficulty with communication and social interaction. A child who is autistic may exhibit repetitive actions (such as flapping of hands or arms).

Autism spectrum disorders(ASD): A series of disorders including autism, pervasive development disorder, and Asperger syndrome.

Background noise: The environmental sounds of a place. In the classroom, background noise might consist of students talking, chairs moving, the rattle of paper, and sounds of the heating and cooling system.

Behavior chart: A personal chart for tracking (and later rewarding) desired behaviors. A behavior chart may be marked with tallies or with stickers.

Centers for Disease Control and Prevention: The government agency that monitors and disseminates information on the prevention and treatment of diseases and disabilities.

Central auditory processing disorder (CAPD): The inability to understand what is heard (such as differences in the beginning sounds of two words or a series of directions).

Central nervous system: The brain and spinal column.

Cerebral palsy: A condition of damage to the motor control centers of the brain, which may result in difficulty with movement, communication, or thinking skills.

Character trait: A behavior pattern (positive or negative). Respect, responsibility, and perseverance are examples of positive character traits.

Cleft palate: An abnormal opening in the upper palate of the mouth.

Cochlear implant: An electronic hearing device that is surgically implanted in the ear. The cochlear implant sends sound to the nerves in the cochlea.

Cognitive: Referring to thinking skills.

Cystic fibrosis: An inherited disease that affects the healthy functioning of the lungs and digestive system.

Developmental delay: An unusual lag in one or more skills of early childhood (communication, movement, behavior, or thinking).

Developmental milestone: The age when most children begin to do a particular skill (such as sitting or saying single words).

Developmental therapy: The education of the infant or young child in communication, thinking, and motor skills.

Disability: A special need resulting from a birth defect, injury, or disease.

Down syndrome: A genetic disability (cognitive and motor) caused by an extra 21st chromosome.

Dwarfism: The condition of being abnormally short (in many cases this is a genetic disorder).

Dyscalcula: A learning disability that affects the ability to understand numbers or to remember and understand math processes.

Dysgraphia: A learning disability that affects writing.

Dyslexia: A learning disability that affects reading.

Early intervention: Therapy and education for infants and toddlers.

Fluctuating hearing loss: A hearing loss that comes and goes due to fluid in the ear.

FM auditory trainer: A hearing device that amplifies the speaker's voice and minimizes background noise in the room.

Galactosemia: A condition caused by the inability to digest galactose (from the lactose found in milk products).

Genetic counseling: Information for prospective parents with a higher risk of having a baby with a birth defect. The risk can be evidenced in family medical history or recognized because of certain conditions of one or both parents.

Genetics: An individual's inheritance of traits, conditions, or disease.

Guide dog: A dog specially trained in leading the blind through safe walking conditions.

Hemophilia: A bleeding or clotting disorder that is inherited or brought on by another illness.

Huntington disease: An inherited neurological disorder that affects movement and results in death.

Inclusion classroom: A regular education classroom that is made up of typically developing students and those with special needs.

Individualized Education Program (IEP): The document that outlines the education plan (goals and services) for students with special needs.

Individualized family service plan (IFSP): The document that outlines the education and therapy plan for babies and toddlers birth to age three with special needs. Emphasis is placed on the family's goals for the child.

Intermediate care facility for the mentally retarded (ICF/MR): An institutional living arrangement for the mentally retarded that includes services such as therapy.

Juvenile arthritis: A condition involving swelling of the joints, which may be temporary or permanent.

Learning disability: A neurological disorder that results in difficulty with reading, writing, and math (including processing and memory).

Legally blind: Having visual acuity of 20/200 or less.

Low vision: Visual acuity less than 20/70 that does not fall in the range of legal blindness.

Marfan syndrome: An inherited condition that affects the connective tissues of the body.

Medicaid: Low-cost (co-pay) health insurance for low-income and some individuals with disabilities.

Meltdown: Emotional upset (including crying and anger) caused by feeling overwhelmed.

Middle ear: An internal part of the ear that can become inflamed and fill with fluid as a result of infection.

Mobility training: Instruction in the safe movement around an area for individuals with low vision or blindness.

Multiple impairments: The condition of having more than one special need, such as being deaf-blind or having ADHD and a physical disability.

Neural tube defect (NTD): A birth defect that involves incomplete formation of the spinal column (spina bifida) or lack of formation of the brain (anencephaly).

Obsessive-compulsive disorder (OCD): An anxiety disorder that is manifested by fixation on a particular thought and repeating certain behaviors. A common OCD behavior is washing and rewashing the hands.

Occupational therapy (OT): Treatment through exercise and prescriptive activities for using the hands to accomplish daily tasks (writing, buttoning, pulling a zipper).

Oppositional defiant disorder (ODD): A behavior disorder characterized by resistance to direction or authority.

Orthopedic disability: A disability that involves the physical structure (bone and muscle) and movement of the body.

Pervasive development disorder (PDD): A behavior disorder involving communication and social interaction. Some repetitive behaviors are related to PDD. PDD is the overall term used to describe a number of disorders on the autism spectrum.

Physical therapy (PT): Exercises and prescriptive activities involving the large muscles used for sitting, standing, and walking.

Preferential seating: Sitting in a place to allow easy sight, hearing, or focus during classroom instruction.

Preferred activity: An activity that a child enjoys doing. Often a preferred activity is used as a reward for completing work or staying on task for a period of time.

Premature baby: A baby born before the thirty-seventh week of gestation.

Residual sight: The functional sight of an individual with low vision or blindness.

Respite care: Temporary care of a child with a disability to allow a physical, mental, and emotional break.

Selective mutism: A communication disorder in which an individual is able and willing to talk in some environments (at home, with friends), but is unwilling to talk in others.

Sensory integration dysfunction: The inability to tolerate or process input from the senses.

Speech milestones: The age when most children demonstrate a particular speech skill (saying particular sounds, saying words in isolation, or using words and phrases to communicate wants and needs).

Spina bifida: A neural tube defect in which the spinal column is not fully enclosed.

Strabismus: A condition in which one eye may point at an angle (wandering eye), or the eyes may point inward (cross-eyed).

Tactile defensivenes: An extreme aversion to the sensation of touch. It may be evidenced by an intolerance of clothing tags or of eating foods with certain textures.

Token reward: A small item or trinket used to reward desired behavior or completion of a task.

Ultrasound: A prenatal screening used to assess the size of the fetus and certain birth defects.

Unilateral hearing loss: A hearing loss involving only one ear.

Vision screening: An initial assessment of visual acuity. A child who fails a vision screening will be referred for a full vision test.

504 plan: The document that outlines needed accommodations for a child with special needs who does not require the direct special education services of an IEP.

Index